What Your Colleagues

Strategic and deliberate approaches to inquiry have been shown to be extremely helpful to educators who seek to ensure that they are meeting the needs of their students. In this important new book, Kimberly Mitchell provides practical insights and methods on how to incorporate inquiry into practice. For educators who seek to enhance their effectiveness and make a difference for all the students they serve, this book will be an invaluable resource and guide.

—**Pedro A. Noguera, PhD, Distinguished Professor of Education**
UCLA Graduate School of Education and Information Studies,
Los Angeles, CA

Mitchell has translated the latest terminology—pedagogical jargon—into lively language and useful advice that will strike a chord for classroom teachers! She gets it.

—**Deborah Meier, Educator and Author**
Coalition of Essential Schools

This is a book that will help you become the inquiry teacher you need to be.

—**Kath Murdoch, Education Consultant, University Lecturer**
Author of *The Power of Inquiry*
Australia

Experience Inquiry is an excellent book for demystifying how to promote inquiry in the classroom. It's also a clarion call for building strong personal bonds between teacher and student. Chapter after chapter emphasizes the extraordinary opportunity teachers have and the practical tools they can use to create an environment in which students' ideas, feelings, and questions are valued.

—**Dan Rothstein, Author**
Make Just One Change: Teach Students
to Ask Their Own Questions

Mitchell has given us a "field guide" to uncover, unpack, and enjoy the nobility that is teaching. Her gift is a joyful discomfort that challenges all of us to better actualize the gifts we pledge to the students we serve . . . best enjoyed in the company of your colleagues.

—**Don Shalvey, Founder, Aspire Public Schools**
Deputy Director K–12 Bill and Melinda Gates Foundation

More than a good, engaging read, Experience Inquiry *is an experiential challenge for educators and educational leaders committed to creating schools where students "do most of the question asking and answer seeking." Kimberly Mitchell has provided a fun, accessible way for all of us to reflect on our own capacity for inquiry and in the process become better listeners and learners—which ultimately makes for better teachers.*

—Susan Enfield, Superintendent
Highline Public Schools
Burien, WA

Are you ready to experience authentic inquiry? Experience Inquiry *takes you on a reflective, inquiry-based learning journey to bring clarity to what educators have wrestled with since John Dewey's time: the nebulousness of "inquiry." Kimberly masterfully engages you in what effective inquiry-based teaching and learning looks like, sounds like, and feels like. Finally, there is a book that actually differentiates for all levels of teaching experience to provide the foundation our newest teachers need while pushing our most experienced inquiry-based teachers to the next level. This is a must read for all teachers, PLCs, and school and district personnel who are working to improve inquiry-based teaching and learning.*

—Bodo Heiliger, Elementary IB Principal
and IBPYP Workshop Leader
Portland, OR

While there is much talk about inquiry-based teaching, Kimberly Mitchell walks the walk in this highly practical, easy-to-read manual for inquiry in 21st century teaching and learning. Unlike most other books on the topic, Mitchell doesn't stop at how to engage in more inquiry-based teaching and learning; she takes the unique step of walking educators through their own inquiry-based self-reflections and evaluations. Some of the best (and most affordable) professional development I have had in a while can be found within these pages; this book will have a permanent place on my go-to education bookshelf.

—Alexis Wiggins, Author
Founder and Director of the Cohort of
Educators for Essential Learning
Woodlands, TX

What a thoughtful and generous book! Experience Inquiry *is an amazing resource for teachers who are curious about bringing inquiry immediately into their classrooms—whether implementing w/their "beginner mind" or improving their daily practice.*

—Kathleen Blakeslee, IB Coordinator
Mark Twain Elementary
Houston, TX

Experience Inquiry is a must-have workbook for new teachers and teachers who want to come to the work anew. It's refreshing to find a book that asks us to pause, think, and reflect for ourselves.

—Colleen Oliver, Vice President—School Leadership
New Teacher Center
Santa Cruz, CA

The shift from "what" and "how to" to "why" and "what if" is a must for 21st century educators, and Experience Inquiry *provides a powerful, but practical framework for any educator to join education's long overdue critical thinking revolution.*

—Colin Seale, Founder of thinkLaw
Glendale, AZ

Kimberly Mitchell is a fabulous teacher and coach who has managed to create in Experience Inquiry *a book as engaging for readers as the classrooms she envisions are for students. It's a must-read if you're looking for support on your path toward helping your students gain the curiosity, understanding, and creativity to shape a better future.*

—Wendy Kopp, Founder, Teach For America and
CEO, Teach For All

This book will help you grow your own ideas about what it means to do inquiry. It will help you learn more about yourself and your students by inviting you to work through a set of thought-provoking and practical exercises. Invite your colleagues along for this journey, and you'll find yourselves taking new steps towards envisioning and creating inquiry-based classrooms.

—Elham Kazemi, Professor
Associate Dean of Professional Learning
University of Washington, Seattle

With skill and grace, Mitchell navigates the important questions that teachers—and all educators—should be asking themselves. Deeply personal, reflective, and inspirational, Experience Inquiry *is a treasure trove of carefully crafted, eminently practical ideas for improving the practice of teaching. Bravo!*

—Ash Vasudeva, Vice President for Strategic Initiatives
Carnegie Foundation for the
Advancement of Teaching

Mitchell's book is honest, and while it could have been full of "eduspeak," it is not. It is real, focused, and to the point. Full of suggestions on how to implement and refine your inquiry practice, this book is inspiring and practical. As a life-long learner myself, this book helped me share in the enthusiasm kids have for learning. From the perspective of a teacher, it's a toolkit we should all make our own!

—Francesca Zammarano, JS Design Tech Teacher
and Technology Integrator
United Nations International School
New York, NY

So many people fancy themselves experts on teaching, but few of them have the wisdom of Kimberly Mitchell. Her ceaseless focus on inquiry and call for teachers to "talk less and ask more" are some of the simplest but powerful pieces of wisdom I've come across in my decade-plus in the classroom.

—Nathan Gibbs-Bowling, 2016 National Teacher
of the Year Finalist, 2014 Milken National Teaching Award
Tacoma, WA

Experience Inquiry *is full of tangible strategies for fostering inquiry with students of any age. Kimberly Mitchell has knocked it out of the park with this book—it's highly readable, accessible, and chock full of great information. I loved the practical exercises that allow you to try as you go. This is a must read for teachers looking to use inquiry-based teaching in the classrooms. Buy this book today and read it with your team.*

—Bonnie Lathram, Writer and Educator
Co-Author of *Smart Parents: Parenting for Powerful Learning*

Kimberly Mitchell has put together a powerful book at a key time in the evolution of how we teach, and how students learn. Central to the purpose of this book is the understanding that creating a culture of inquiry begins with the teacher. Many educators know this, but may not have had the opportunity, or the guidance, to really explore what this means for them, their habits, and their practices. This book does just that. Writing in a friendly and informal style, Mitchell invites us to be introspective and to really ponder who we are as educators in this critical time, a time when traditional teaching habits need to be rapidly replaced with those that promote student choice, decision-making, and empowerment. With a rich variety of anecdotes, examples, wisdom, and practical-thinking tools and strategies, Experience Inquiry *is a must-have for the 21st century educator.*

—Sam Sherratt, Time Space Education
International Schools Consultant

Experience Inquiry

Everything that needs to be said has already been said.

But since no one was listening, everything must be said again.

—Andrew Paul Guillaume Gide
French Author and Nobel Laureate

Experience Inquiry

5 Powerful Strategies,
50 Practical Experiences

Kimberly L. Mitchell

Foreword by Kath Murdoch, Author of *The Power of Inquiry*

CORWIN
A SAGE Publishing Company

FOR INFORMATION:

Corwin
A SAGE Company
2455 Teller Road
Thousand Oaks, California 91320
(800) 233-9936
www.corwin.com

SAGE Publications Ltd.
1 Oliver's Yard
55 City Road
London EC1Y 1SP
United Kingdom

SAGE Publications India Pvt. Ltd.
B 1/I 1 Mohan Cooperative Industrial Area
Mathura Road, New Delhi 110 044
India

SAGE Publications Asia-Pacific Pte. Ltd.
3 Church Street
#10-04 Samsung Hub
Singapore 049483

Acquisitions Editor: Ariel Bartlett Curry
Development Editor: Desirée A. Bartlett
Editorial Assistant: Jessica Vidal
Production Editor: Amy Schroller
Copy Editor: Lana Todorovic-Arndt
Typesetter: C&M Digitals (P) Ltd.
Proofreader: Jennifer Grubba
Indexer: Sheila Bodell
Cover Designer: Scott Van Atta
Marketing Manager: Margaret O'Connor

Printed in the United States of America

ISBN 978-1-5443-1712-0

This book is printed on acid-free paper.

SUSTAINABLE FORESTRY INITIATIVE

Certified Chain of Custody
Promoting Sustainable Forestry
www.sfiprogram.org
SFI-01268

SFI label applies to text stock

18 19 20 21 22 10 9 8 7 6 5 4 3 2 1

CONTENTS

Visit the companion website at **https://www
.inquirypartners.com/** for downloadable resources.

FOREWORD

Over 30 years ago, in my 3rd year of undergraduate studies, our tutor took us on a field trip to the zoo. We were all a little puzzled as to how a trip to the zoo could possibly help us learn "how to teach," but as it turned out, this day was a truly transformative moment in my career. That trip to the zoo set me on the inquiry path I have travelled ever since.

Our day at the zoo began with a lesson in the Education Centre. But this was unlike any lesson I had ever experienced. In an environment deliberately designed to cultivate curiosity and invite wonder, Frank Ryan (a young teacher who went on to become a leader in environmental education in Australia) lit a spark in us all. I don't recall him saying much—but I do recall the beautiful corn snake I held, the magic and intrigue of a collection of rare stick insects, and the conversations he facilitated about our connection to the animals with which we share the planet. And I recall my thirst to find out more. Frank inspired in us a yearning to investigate. We moved out into the zoo that day with eager hearts and heads filled with questions. Suddenly *we* were the researchers—the zoologists, the scientists, the designers, and conservationists. We had theories to test, problems to solve, information to gather, and ideas to grow.

We were experiencing inquiry.

I knew then, that I wanted to be *that* kind of teacher. I wanted to be someone who could teach without telling, someone who would truly listen to students and encourage them to think deeply. I wanted to be someone who knew how to combine the right experience with the right questions to engage the learner. I wanted to be someone who truly valued curiosity, who modelled it, and someone who would let students *own* their learning. What I didn't know then was that I wanted to be what I now identify as an "inquiry teacher."

It took several years for me to connect theories of teaching and learning with what my gut told me was this powerful way to "be" in the classroom. It took a long time to build a repertoire of practices that would effectively inspire inquiry. What a gift Kimberly Mitchell's book would have been at the time! I am so thrilled by the contribution this book will make to the field. This is a book that will help you become the inquiry teacher you need to be.

Despite the persistent type-casting of the inquiry teacher as a structure averse, hands-off, "guide on the side," true inquiry learning in schools is most often a consequence of carefully planned, thoughtful, and highly sophisticated moves made by teachers. My experience as a student in the zoo that day did not simply happen because of the compelling environment and subject matter. It was powerful because of the way the *teacher* provoked, supported, and deftly facilitated my learning. Building the capacity to work this way is complex and challenging work. No "program" can do it, and there is no recipe or step-by-step guide. To truly transform ourselves and shed the tired skin of traditional teaching, we need to engage in challenging experiences ourselves. *We* need to inquire. As Kimberly says, "Most critically, you have to engage in inquiry yourself to truly understand it."

The role of key practices for nurturing inquiry is receiving growing attention in my own work. It is always exciting when you discover that someone on the other side of the world is unearthing similar ideas to your own. Kimberly's five, elegant practices echo the same kind of pedagogies we are witnessing in effective inquiry classrooms here in Australia. Inquiry learning is best nurtured by teachers who talk less and ask more, who stay curious, get personal, encourage evidence, and extend thinking time. This deceptively simple collection ("The Inquiry Five") is the perfect pedagogical toolkit for teachers who know it is time to re-think their routine ways of working, but perhaps do not yet know how.

At its heart, inquiry is an approach that positions and values the learner as an active, responsible, and capable partner in the teaching–learning transaction. The approach is unashamedly constructivist with its central tenet being to honor the learner's right to "do the learning for themselves." As Kimberly states in her own definition, it is about giving students every opportunity to do their own question asking and answer seeking.

In the 50 suggestions for ways to build our understanding and repertoire of practice, this book reflects the complexity and depth of the inquiry approach, while remaining beautifully clear and invitational. The work is well evidenced without being weighed down by too much theorizing. In fact, reading through this book is like having one of those breathless, energizing conversations we cherish when we get talking with a great teacher buddy. Literally and figuratively, the author speaks directly to us as teachers and to the heart of why we do what we do. The wisdom of Kimberly's own experience as an inquiring educator infuses every page. In the spirit of the true inquiry teacher, her heart is on her sleeve as she leads by example and shares with honesty and passion the real power of the approach. It's not often I describe a teacher-resource book as a real "page-turner," but this one is.

I guarantee you will visit this book again and again not only for the many wonderful ideas it offers, but for the real warmth, wit, and the wisdom with which Kimberly communicates her message. I urge you to take that message seriously and to embrace the challenge within these chapters. Traditional, transmission models of teaching are well and truly past their use-by date. The young people with whom we work deserve nothing less than teachers who see them as capable and curious inquirers and who instill in them a joyful hunger to question, investigate, and "make meaning" throughout their lives.

They deserve to experience inquiry.

Kath Murdoch
Teacher, Author, Consultant

ACKNOWLEDGMENTS

None of this would be possible without my students. Whether we worked together in Inglewood, Compton, East Los Angeles, Quito, Ecuador, Seattle, Athens, Greece or Buenos Aires, Argentina, know that you were more than just my student; you were also my teacher. Thank you.

The following teachers and education leaders have inspired me throughout the last 27 years: Jackie Cochran, Nat Smith, Queena Kim, C. Allison Jack, Amy Wendel, Natalie Rollhaus Burton, Rich Polio, Ben Kramer, Kevin Burns, Ann Hickey, Tom Bailey, Jane Mantarakis, Steve Medeiros, Stamatis Vokos, Kathleen Blakeslee, Paula Baxter, Janet Blanford, Colleen Oliver, Jodi Haavig, Kathie Tourangeau, Maru Albarracín, Oscar Ghillione, Agustina Blanco, Ashley Olinger, Erin Collins Gustafson, Nate Gibbs-Bowling, Mia Tuan, Tom Stritikus, Sophia Sinco, Morva McDonald, Elham Kazemi, Susan Enfield, Tony Byrd, Sara Morris, Martin Piccoli, Aubree Gomez, Danielle Warman, Erica Baba, Francesca Zammarano, Sharon Kriscovich, Julie Kalmus, Emily McGrath, Pat Hughes, Laura McCarthy, and Barry Hoonan.

Author and 'Geek Momma' Lynn Brunelle held my hand and magic-wanded my writing. She is dynamite in every way.

Several trusted colleagues read through my manuscripts and provided me with just the right mix of critical edits and ebullient praise: Jill Lubow, Stacy Kaner Pipson, Misty Paterson, Leslie Maniotes, Nicky Bourgeois, Kira Hicks Blonsky, Sarah L'Hoir, Kath Murdoch, Stacey Runstad Campbell, Scottie Nash, Dan Finkel, Maggie Chumbley, Katleiah Ramos, and Lara Lyons. Thank you so much.

Ariel Bartlett Curry, my editor at Corwin, instantly connected with the content and patiently guided me through the process.

My sisters, both compelling writers, Jen Lasher Breen and Heidi Lasher Schaub, carefully reviewed drafts. Most importantly, they offer me unconditional sister love.

Finally, thank you to my family for allowing me to sit for hours with my laptop and a faraway look in my eyes, relatively undisturbed. I love you Tim, Zoe and Van.

PUBLISHER'S ACKNOWLEDGMENTS

Corwin gratefully acknowledges the contributions of the following reviewers:

Sandra E. Archer, District Classroom Management Coach
Volusia County Schools
Deland, Florida

Carol S. Holzberg, Director of Technology
Greenfield Public Schools
Greenfield, Massachusetts

Saundra Mouton, International Baccalaureate
Charter school
Houston, Texas

Michelle Strom, Middle School Language Arts Teacher
Riley Middle School
Fort Riley, Kansas

Ernie Rambo, Grade 7, U.S. History Teacher
Walter Johnson Academy of International Studies
Las Vegas, Nevada

Mandy White, Grade 7, Science Teacher
Fort Riley Middle School
Fort Riley, Kansas

Margie Zamora, K–5 Digital Learning Coach
Elaine Wynn Elementary School, Clark County School District
Las Vegas, Nevada

ABOUT THE AUTHOR

Kimberly L. Mitchell is co-founder of Inquiry Partners, a global professional learning organization dedicated to promoting inquiry-based teaching strategies. She also teaches several undergraduate courses at the University of Washington's College of Education. Kimberly received her BA in history and philosophy from Skidmore College and her MA in administration and policy analysis from Stanford University. She lives in Seattle, WA, with her husband and two children.

Dedicated to the finest question askers I know:

Mom and Dad

INTRODUCTION

Inquiry-based instruction sounds complicated but is deceptively simple. Inquiry is teaching in such a way that the students are doing most of the work. They are asking questions. They are researching complex problems. They are formulating opinions. They are even at times teaching and offering feedback. Inquiry works at every grade level and in every subject area.

Given constraints of the traditional school model, *implementing* inquiry is the tricky part. Plenty of books will be able to tell you the benefits of inquiry, the research behind inquiry, and even processes to follow in the context of a subject area. But that's not enough. Implementing inquiry involves changing beliefs about the teacher and student roles in the classroom. It involves dispositional shifts as well as procedural ones. Most critically, it requires us as teachers to engage in inquiry ourselves.

> **The purpose of this book is to offer you inquiry experiences so that you can teach in an inquiry-based way.**

When my son asks, "How do I play like Messi?" he's not looking for a biomechanical explanation of how to play like the soccer phenom. He wants to *play*! This book offers you the same: the opportunity to *do* inquiry as you read about it.

You may be thinking, "Yeah, thanks for that, but I'd rather just read a book about inquiry. Just tell me what to do!" I get it. Reading is easier. It's more comfortable and less time-consuming. It doesn't require you to put on your shoes, reorganize your schedule, or talk with others. But like listening to a lecture, it's not as effective either. It's a lot like Jell-O; we may be moved (or wiggled) but remain essentially unchanged. Even the most insightful books and dynamic workshops will fade from memory over time. Rarely do they translate into deep, long-lasting behavioral changes.

Real change in how we teach, not just occasionally, but *essentially*, will require all of us to get out of our seats and comfort zones. It will require us to move and *be moved*. Roll your eyes. But you know it's necessary. Are you ready?

CHAPTER 1

WHAT IS INQUIRY?

You weren't expecting a book on inquiry-based learning to answer this question *for* you, were you? While it's tempting to turn this question back on you, the reader, inquiry isn't only about asking questions. Inquiry is also about exploring answers. Besides, leaving simple questions unanswered is irritating and often irresponsible.

Here's how I define inquiry:

> Inquiry is a way of being (a disposition) and a way of teaching (a pedagogy) that gets the students to do most of the question asking and answer seeking. The role of the teacher is to design and guide experiences (and an environment) that promote student discussions, collaboration, and critical thinking. Inquiry methods enhance relationships and breathe joyful curiosity into classrooms.

A few notes about my definition of inquiry:

- I use *inquiry* as shorthand throughout this book for *inquiry-based teaching and learning*.
- Inquiry is closely related to and often synonymous with *active, student-centered, constructivist, discovery,* and *experiential* learning.
- There are different levels of teacher involvement in inquiry (*guided, structured, free, open*). While these are interesting to learn about and study, they are not essential to know to start implementing inquiry.

- The inquiry method of teaching and the *scientific method* are related, but not synonymous. Inquiry requires *a way of being* in the classroom, in addition to *at times* following a set of processes, such as the scientific method.

- Knowing what inquiry is will get you a definition you can use in a staff meeting, but it won't help you change your instruction. In other words, don't stop here!

My Own Inquiry Journey

I am a former teacher, principal, grant-maker, new teacher trainer, workshop presenter, school authorizer, consultant, adjunct professor, and app developer. Blech. I'm a teacher, simple as that. Today, I spend most of my time teaching undergraduates at a large research university in the college of education. I started my professional journey in education in 1991, when I accepted the keys to my fifth-grade classroom at Worthington Elementary in Los Angeles, California. I never looked back. Teaching hooked me from the start.

There isn't much in the education field that I haven't dipped my toes in. Over the years, I've felt both heart-soaringly accomplished and shamefully inept in my work with children and adults. I still do. Teaching is where I feel at home. I find it to be the most challenging, creative, and complex work there is.

I had to leave teaching for many years to realize this, however.

At one point in my career, I worked as a consultant for the International Baccalaureate (IB). For those unfamiliar with IB, it's a global curriculum, instruction, and assessment program centered on inquiry. It was my job to travel to schools around the United States and Canada sharing the IB program and authorizing new schools. I was a former IB principal and found it easy to be enthusiastic about it. I loved the program (still do).

One afternoon, I stood before a large group of teachers inside a carpeted double-wide classroom situated on the hot asphalt of a sprawling California elementary school. A noisy AC blasted cool air over the heads of 40 exhausted teachers at the end of a school day. They (or their administration, I couldn't be sure which) were interested in implementing IB.

I moved quickly through curriculum and assessment components and was reassured by a couple nodding heads. Most of this seemed to make sense to this seasoned crew, even though the looks on their faces were resigned and weary. Then, we got to the instruction component. I started with "IB teachers teach in an 'inquiry-based way.'"

Cue the record-scratch. "*Inquiry—what?!*"

A teacher at the back of the room spoke up first: "I don't understand what inquiry is, and I'm too tired to read through research. Can you just *show us* what inquiry looks like in a real classroom—like, mine?" she asked. The AC clicked off, uncomfortable silence filled the room.

It was the right question to ask; I just wasn't prepared for it. I stammered something about Dewey's research (1938), promised to locate some videos they could watch, and made a mental note to search for classroom transcripts.

Although I was a huge fan of inquiry on an intellectual level, I couldn't claim to have ever been an inquiry practitioner myself. I could convincingly speak about it, generally define it, and cite the research. I'd even observed great inquiry teachers in action on occasion. But had I ever really led an inquiry-based classroom myself? Um, nope.

How could I explain inquiry in a way that teachers could understand, without having ever done it myself? Could I even identify what made an inquiry classroom different from a traditional one? How could I possibly demonstrate it? Was I even qualified to do this? Was I selling snake oil?

I searched furiously for videos of great inquiry teachers and came up short. This was 2004, and YouTube and the Teaching Channel didn't exist yet.

How could I expect teachers to try something different if I wasn't willing to do it myself?

I remember making up some excuse about not knowing enough content or not having the right context for demonstrating inquiry properly. But that was a cop-out. I needed to put on my big-girl pants and get back down to that school and simply try my best. It was going to be up to me to step up to the challenge of demonstrating inquiry.

After some hand-wringing, that's what I did. I returned to this California elementary school 6 months later and demonstrated inquiry-based lessons in five different classrooms with the teachers watching. No, they weren't perfect lessons. But yes, they made an impression and provoked the right kinds of conversations. The teachers got something from watching inquiry in action with their own students and were now willing to give it a shot themselves. I got a taste of what it felt like to be an inquiry teacher.

That was 15 years ago. I've been on the road ever since.

That honest and straight-shooting teacher's question changed the course of my professional life. In the many years since that day in California, I've completely immersed myself in the world of practical, real-life inquiry-based instruction. I've become even more convinced that inquiry should be the default way we teach every subject and every learner.

It's not snake oil.

I've traveled around the world demonstrating inquiry lessons inside classrooms, simulating inquiry lessons at staff meetings, coaching inquiry lessons in real-time, filming inquiry lessons, and most of all, admiring great inquiry lessons and the people who teach them. These teachers are the real life-changers out there, for no student (or teacher) ever walks away from a great inquiry lesson without being profoundly impacted.

Inquiry really works to restore joy and curiosity inside our classrooms, not only for our students, but for teachers as well. There is plenty of research to support its efficacy (even when students are confronted with very "non-inquiry" standardized tests). The challenge is really in understanding how to implement it in a practical way. That's what this book is all about; answering the question, "How do I implement inquiry?"

EXPERIENCE #1

Inquiry Self-Survey

Are you *already* teaching in an inquiry-based way? Maybe! Read through the statements below and mark an "X" where you would honestly put yourself and your students on this continuum (0 = absolutely not true [yet] to 10 = unequivocally true). The further to the right, the more inquiry-based you are. Try not to overthink this or beat yourself up with this survey. We're *all* on a continuum!

. . . .

1 I have a strong relationship with each one of my students.

0 _____ 10

2 I am OK not having all the answers.

0 _____ 10

3 My students talk (academically) as much, or more, than I do.

0 _____ 10

4 There is equal verbal participation between students in my classroom.

0 _____ 10

5 I ask more questions than make statements while teaching.

0 _____ 10

6 My students ask at least as many questions as I do during class.

0 ——————————————————————————————————— 10

7 Students listen to other students when they speak. I rarely repeat or paraphrase for them.

0 ——————————————————————————————————— 10

8 Students back up their claims and cite their sources without prompting.

0 ——————————————————————————————————— 10

9 Students have lots of opportunities to make their own choices in my classroom.

0 ——————————————————————————————————— 10

10 There are lots of opportunities for students to quietly think and reflect.

0 ——————————————————————————————————— 10

· ·

online resources ⟍ Available for download at **https://www.inquirypartners.com/**

Well done! For now, set this aside. Let it marinate. We will return to it later.

2

BEGINNING YOUR INQUIRY JOURNEY

We've all been there; that moment when someone asks you to do something you know is probably good for you, but you *just don't wanna!* Maybe it's an early morning run, a visit to the dentist, or having a difficult conversation. Perhaps it's this book. My colleague at Inquiry Partners, Maggie Chumbley, calls this the "groan zone." It's a bit like Vygotsky's Zone of Proximal Development: that sweet spot of not too easy and not too hard. The groan zone is a nice stretch that yields results. This book will offer you an opportunity to regularly move into your groan zone. (See Figure 2.1 on the following page.)

Notice that the groan zone stops before that space called the panic zone. The panic zone is where there is so much stress that learning becomes nearly impossible. When children arrive to school already in the panic zone, bringing them to the comfort zone should be our first priority.

Think for a minute: *How often do you require your students to get into the groan zone? When is the last time you were in the groan zone?*

How to Use This Book

As you can see, there isn't a lot of reading to do in this book. There is a lot of *space for writing*, however. Inquiry classrooms are full of metaphorical blank spaces. Filling in the literal blanks in this book is a great way to ease into space-filling and to get conversations going with your colleagues and students.

FIGURE 2.1 ■ The groan zone is where the most powerful learning happens.

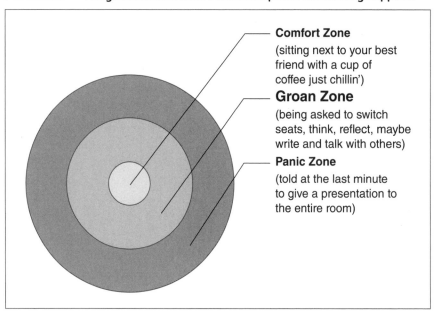

Comfort Zone
(sitting next to your best friend with a cup of coffee just chillin')

Groan Zone
(being asked to switch seats, think, reflect, maybe write and talk with others)

Panic Zone
(told at the last minute to give a presentation to the entire room)

This book is meant to be written and doodled in, drawn on, pulled apart, folded up, and spilled upon. Play with it. Flip through it. Start anywhere. Go in sequence or skip around. Try the exercises on your own, with your colleagues, and in your classroom with students. Let your hair down. Flip upside down and see things from a new perspective. Chances are, this book will become so beloved, because ultimately it's *your creation.*

Some of the experiences you will enjoy, and others may have you searching for excuses to hide in the bathroom or disinfect student desks. That's good. Pay close attention to those, especially. Oftentimes, the most challenging experiences are the ones that bring about the most growth and transformation.

I've structured these 50 experiences around five key strategies that will help you understand and implement inquiry in your own classroom. It's low on word count and high on thinking space.

This book will ask something from you, too.

Like in an inquiry classroom, space and power is shared within the pages of this book. The book is designed not to *tell* you what inquiry is, but to *invite* you to discover it for yourself.

You will be invited to think, ask questions, experiment, create, write, and share. You will need to periodically reach for a pen, move your body, make time for a conversation, ask for release time, visit classrooms, collect data, record yourself, and reflect. By nudging yourself into the groan zone and engaging in these 50 experiences, you will create a solid inquiry practice.

Even if you're still skeptical about inquiry (*especially* if you're skeptical about inquiry), working through these experiences will improve your relationships with students and colleagues, reduce your workload by placing more demand on students, and breathe new joy into your classroom. Your time will not be wasted if you approach it with an open mind and a willingness to learn.

WITH YOUR COLLEAGUES

I believe strongly in the power of teacher communities of practice. When teachers can work with and learn from one another, they are unstoppable. Most of these experiences are therefore designed for groups of teachers to use in a workshop setting, staff meetings, and/or in professional learning communities (PLCs). The exercises are designed knowing that this time together is precious, limited, and rarely catered (sadly).

WITH YOUR STUDENTS

Many of the experiences within these pages are also perfect for developing stronger bonds between you and your students. Adapt some of the experiences for your content area, tinker with the developmental requirements, and see how your students approach them!

ON YOUR OWN

Use these experiences as personal exploration. No one has to see what you write down. This is *your* workbook. Have at it without worry. Just remember that many of the experiences may require you to work with others, too. Sorry, no getting around this one. We are social animals. Finally, remember that it's the conversations that are sparked from these exercises, not necessarily the exercises themselves, that will create the magic.

Tips for Success

While you are free to romp around these pages on your own, there are experiences that will require you to engage with others. For these, I suggest the following norms:

BE OPEN.

Like heroes from mythology, your journey isn't really complete until you've reflected upon and shared it with others. You'll need to agree to dig into this book on your own *and* with others. Be open to learning something new and deepening your knowledge. In other words, approach this book the same way you'd expect your students to approach what you teach: with a curious mind.

PLAY NICE.

Playing nice means different things to different people. At the very least, have a discussion about what "playing nice" means to you. Establish some ground rules, or norms. I know, norms can be annoying. We're adults and we should know by now how to work together, right? You may be the most well-oiled professional team on the planet, but you still need norms. Review the ones you've already established or create new ones and then guide a conversation about them. Review and post them. Refer back to them frequently. Seriously, you need norms.

COME PREPARED.

When the book calls for group work, make sure your facilitator is not only capable and confident, but also prepared. Even the best activities will bomb with off-the-cuff planning and poor facilitation. Set aside the time needed to think through the possible reactions and outcomes of these experiences before they are enacted. I'm a fan of structured protocols or ways of facilitating group conversations. Check out Liberating Structures and the National Reform Faculty for a treasure trove of ideas.

"LEADERSHIP AND LEARNING ARE INDISPENSABLE TO EACH OTHER."

–JOHN F. KENNEDY, FORMER U.S. PRESIDENT

What's the Role of Administration?

Even if your principal isn't wandering in and out of classrooms or high-fiving students during lunch, his or her vision reverberates in a thousand ways—down the hallways and into the classrooms.

There were two school leaders in my career who modeled inquiry leadership for me: Jackie Cochran and Tom Bailey. Jackie was my elementary school principal in Compton, California, in the early 1990s. Born and raised in Compton, Jackie knew her community inside and out. She embraced its changing demographics at that time, from an African-American suburb of Los Angeles to a Mexican-American one. Jackie learned to speak Spanish, and when she wanted her teachers to try something new, she'd try it first. Jackie was the only principal whom I actually observed *teaching*. Her courage and willingness to be vulnerable like this made a huge impact on me.

Tom Bailey was my high school principal in Seattle, Washington. Tom believed strongly in establishing personal relationships with his students, teachers, and staff. These relationships, he insisted, made it possible for him to make tough calls. Students loved seeing him in the hallways every day because his goal was to know each one of our 1,300 by name. If he couldn't remember someone's name, he paid them a dollar. Tom couldn't afford *not* to know his students by name! Every Friday, when teachers and staff met for drinks after school, Tom would tell me, a young Assistant Principal at the time, "You need to show up. Have one drink, so they think you're human. Then, say goodbye before they *know* you're human."

Who are the administrators you look up to as a teacher? What is it about their leadership that inspires you? Jot down some anecdotes below and share with others.

Optional Experience: Chances are your leadership team is actively involved in supporting inquiry schoolwide (especially if they invested in this book). However, just in case there is reluctance, brainstorm ideas on how you and your colleagues might encourage your leadership team to use the Self-Reflection Tool and administer the Staff Reflection Survey.

Hello, school leader! Your role in successful inquiry implementation is absolutely key. These exercises and strategies apply to you, too. Take a look at the questions below and reflect. Where are you right now in supporting inquiry to flourish schoolwide?

THE INQUIRY LEADER SELF-REFLECTION TOOL

INQUIRY STRATEGIES	QUESTIONS TO REFLECT ON
Get personal.	How well do you know your staff?
	How well does your staff know you?
	What are the rituals in place to strengthen staff relationships?
My Reflections:	
Stay curious.	How do you model the practices you hope to see in classrooms?
	How often do you get into classrooms to guest or co-teach?
	How comfortable are you not knowing the answer to something?
My Reflections:	

(Continued)

INQUIRY STRATEGIES	QUESTIONS TO REFLECT ON
Ask more, talk less.	How much do you talk (vs. your staff) during meetings? How do your meetings with staff encourage question asking?

My Reflections:

Encourage evidence.	How often do you back up your claims? How often does your staff back up their claims? How often do you as a staff rigorously analyze the validity of information or data that comes to you?

My Reflections:

Extend thinking time.	How do you seek and vigorously protect time for your teachers to work together? How often do you release teachers to observe other classrooms?

My Reflections:

 Available for download at **https://www.inquirypartners.com/**

How well do your perceptions square with reality? Offer this survey to your teaching staff (feel free to edit the statements). Ask them to reflect periodically on your leadership as they deepen their inquiry practice.

Once you receive them back, take some time to analyze the results (make sure you are in the right frame of mind to do so first). What seems to be going well and what needs more attention? Refer to the Self-Reflection Tool questions to help you create an action plan.

Staff Reflection Survey

Read through the statements below and mark an "X" depending upon your level of agreement: 0 = absolutely not true (yet) to 10 = unequivocally true.

. . . .

1 I have a strong, positive relationship with my principal.

0 _____ 10

2 Our school has meaningful rituals that build community among teachers.

0 _____ 10

3 I'm motivated to do my best work at this school.

0 _____ 10

4 My principal provides opportunities for us to observe each other teaching.

0 _____ 10

5 My principal models inquiry practice in meetings and workshops.

0 _____ 10

6 My principal prioritizes and protects teacher collaboration time.

0 _____ 10

7 Teachers are equally listened to.

0 _____ 10

8 Our principal backs up his or her claims with evidence.

0 _____ 10

9 Teachers have lots of opportunities to give input and make choices.

0 _____ 10

10 Our principal offers regular opportunities for teachers to think and reflect.

0 _____ 10

· ·

online resources ⌐ Available for download at **https://www.inquirypartners.com/**

I wish my principal knew:

The Importance of Balance and Harmony

One of my favorite snacks is "Chicago Mix" popcorn. This delicious and slightly addicting concoction is simply cheddar cheese and caramel-covered popcorn all mixed together. It achieves that perfect sweet and yet salty "umami" taste. But there is a trick to eating it. If you grab a handful of just cheese or a handful of just caramel, it doesn't achieve the balance that makes it so great. There's a perfect ratio for every Chicago Mix eater. For me, it's three cheese to every one caramel. That's my harmonious balance.

It's the same with inquiry. You need a mix of activities to achieve balance and harmony in the classroom. Too much lecturing is boring. Too many questions without answers is confusing. Too much freedom in the classroom is chaotic. And too many projects without real content and skill-building is frustrating.

Remember that becoming an inquiry-based teacher doesn't mean you swing the pendulum wildly to one side or another without warning. It's not an "all or nothing." It means you are willing to *mix up your strategies* and achieve balance and harmony with your activities and approaches.

3

TAKING STOCK OF YOUR CLASSROOM

Engaging in the exercises in this book will not only help with your inquiry practice, but it will also renew your teaching spirit. Check any box below that applies to you right now:

. . . .

☐ I'm working harder than most of my students.

☐ The majority of my students care more about their grades than about learning.

☐ I've lost sight of who I am and why I'm teaching.

☐ I'm thinking of quitting the teaching profession.

. . . .

If you checked at least one box, you're heading in the right direction! Keep going. This book is designed for you.

If you haven't checked a box, your *colleagues need you* to work alongside these exercises with them.

EXPERIENCE #2

How Do You Know If You're "Doing" Inquiry?

The most common reaction I receive from teachers after an inquiry workshop is: "I'm just relieved that I'm *already* doing these things!" This is a reasonable reaction for many of us who work hard without a lot of feedback and pats on the back. Reassurance feels good. But it can be misleading, too.

The truth is that most teachers are *not* already doing these things. Think about it. If we were, our classrooms and schools would look very different than they do today. We wouldn't be making documentaries about progressive schools. I'm sure your classroom is the exception, but let's make sure we are being completely honest with ourselves.

Awareness and acceptance is the first step to creating an inquiry classroom. It means asking yourself what is happening beyond the grades, test scores, and formal evaluations. It means taking in feedback from the most difficult student or parent. Nobody is perfect, so take that pressure off yourself. Above all, try not to take it personally. This is simply about realizing that we are often unconsciously defaulting back to teaching habits that are counter-productive to what we are really going for in our classrooms. It's OK. It happens. You're OK. You're human.

Inquiry teachers are curious people, and so their disposition is one of wonder rather than all-knowing. They are willing to be wrong. They embrace mistakes as the best methods for learning. They are open to new and sometimes conflicting points of view. More than anything, they are honest about where they are and where they want to improve.

ARE YOU READY FOR SOME HONESTY?

Go back to your Self Survey (Experience #1). Read through the statements again. Did you put your X in the right place? Move it if you need to. Find a partner and talk about the statements and your responses. Are you feeling ambivalent or concerned about any of them? Maybe you want to rewrite the survey to represent your instructional goals more completely. Do it!

Next, write down recent specific *examples* from your classroom next to each statement to illustrate *why* you placed the X where you did.

Finally, brainstorm ways in which you can collect data (it doesn't have to be quantitative) to get a better sense of how you're doing with each of these statements. Talk with colleagues about their responses. Which statements do you feel most confident about? What questions does this experience raise for you? There is no need to create an action plan for this right now (unless you're motivated to). Just simply become more aware.

EVIDENCE OF INQUIRY

STATEMENTS	EXAMPLES
I have a strong relationship with each one of my students.	
I am OK not having all the answers.	
My students talk (academically) as much, or more, than I do.	
There is equal verbal participation between students in my classroom.	
I ask more questions than make statements while teaching.	
My students ask at least as many questions as I do during class.	
Students listen to other students when they speak. I rarely repeat or paraphrase for them.	
Students back up their claims and cite their sources without prompting.	
Students have lots of opportunities to make their own choices.	
There are lots of opportunities for students to quietly think and reflect.	

 Available for download at **https://www.inquirypartners.com/**

	POSSIBLE DATA COLLECTION METHODS

EXPERIENCE #3

What Do Your Students Think?

As a university teacher, I receive detailed feedback from my students about my teaching at the end of each quarter. Students are invited to respond to a series of multiple-choice questions and short answer questions. This is collected, computer analyzed, and returned to me along with their written responses within a few days. My students' feedback is worth its weight in gold. They are the ones I care most about impressing. Plus, they are also in the best position to tell me if my teaching is having an impact on their learning experience.

Great, right? Don't you wish this was standard practice in our K–12 schools? Just for your own eyes, you know? The good news is that you don't have to wait for your school or district to act to get regular feedback from your students.

YOU CAN DO IT RIGHT NOW.

Set aside 15 minutes and invite your students to indicate their agreement with statements about their experience in your classroom. I've provided one for you to use right away (Inquiry Student Survey). Make sure it's anonymous so that students won't be afraid to be completely honest.

At the bottom of every survey, offer optional space for students to share their response to the following prompt: *I wish my teacher knew . . .* Students interpret this prompt in a variety of ways, but I always find it incredibly instructive (thanks to Kyle Schwartz, a Colorado distinguished teacher for sharing this idea).

As with the Inquiry Self-Survey, feel free to alter and edit as needed for your purposes. You can create your own student survey by starting with a list of the questions you have about your teaching practice. What information could your students provide that would most help you improve? List some ideas in the space provided.

What I want to know from my students.

Inquiry Student Survey

Reflect on the statements below and show your agreement by marking an "X" on the continuum: 0 = not true to 10 = yes, absolutely.

. . . .

1 I know every student in my class really well.

0 _____ 10

2 My teacher knows me well.

0 _____ 10

3 Students talk more than the teacher in class (about stuff related to the class).

0 _____ 10

4 My teacher asks a lot of really good questions.

0 _____ 10

5 I ask a lot of questions in this class.

0 _____ 10

6 Students get to make a lot of choices in this class.

0 _____ 10

7 My teacher admits to not knowing all the answers.

0 _____ 10

8 Students listen to other students when they speak in this class.

0 _____ 10

9 We spend time talking about where our information comes from.

0 _____ 10

10 I'm learning a lot in this class.

0 _____ 10

. . . .

online resources — Available for download at **https://www.inquirypartners.com/**

I wish my teacher knew:

Reading Your Student Surveys

After you've collected the student surveys, take a moment to pat yourself on the back. This is an intensely personal, emotional, and complex profession. The simple act of asking for and receiving feedback is heroic. My advice for making sense of the feedback is to start with the "I wish my teacher knew" section. Compile these short answers into categories (compliments, advice, questions, concerns). Then, use a blank template to record the approximate placement of the X's for each one of the ten statements. Where do they cluster? Where is there the most and the least agreement? Remember, no self-flagellation allowed. We are all still learning. Go easy on yourself, but keep your eyes open, too.

I WISH MY TEACHER KNEW . . .

COMPLIMENTS

_____

ADVICE

_____

QUESTIONS

_____

CONCERNS

Statement that had the most agreement:

Statement that had the least agreement:

 Available for download at **https://www.inquirypartners.com/**

EXPERIENCE #4

What Do Others See in Your Classroom?

Invite a trusted colleague to come into your classroom for at least 30 minutes. If this colleague accepts the invitation, make sure you are both clear on *what* you want feedback on, *when* you want it, and *how* you want it communicated. This will help mitigate hurt feelings. When we open our classroom doors to others, it tends to get personal.

Use the prompts below to get clear on what you want to know and plan the logistics. Check out the Inquiry Peer Observation Methods as you think about ways to collect data.

1) What do you want feedback on, and why?

2) Who would you feel comfortable inviting into your classroom? Write their name(s) below.

3) Is this a one-time event, or do you want to schedule regular feedback sessions? Write down your plan for scheduling below and how you will coordinate.

4) Do you want to design your own tool to collect data based on what you wrote above? If so, share your thoughts below.

5) Think about what would be the most comfortable way to receive feedback (i.e., in person, video recording, in writing, over coffee, with another person present).

6) When would you like to receive feedback from the observation (i.e. the same day, within a couple days, a week)?

7) Can you return the favor? Who might you approach? Write their name below.

Peer Observation Planning Worksheet

INQUIRY PEER OBSERVATION METHODS

LOOK FOR'S	DATA COLLECTION METHODS
Get Personal Where do you see emotional connections (teacher–student, student–student, and everyone–content) happening?	• Count all the times the teacher uses students' names and/or students use each other's names. • Note when you hear a story or a connection being made between the content and students' lives. • Note body language of students (are they facing only the teacher, or are they clearly listening to one another?).
Stay Curious How does the teacher communicate that he or she is still learning, too?	• Write examples of teacher asking questions they don't have the answer to already. • Note the times when teacher turns questions back on students to discuss and think about rather than giving an answer. • Write verbatim how teacher responds when student gives an answer.

LOOK FOR'S	DATA COLLECTION METHODS
Ask More, Talk Less Who is doing most of the talking and question asking?	• Calculate the talk time (teachers–students–specific student). • Write verbatim all the questions asked during the lesson (and by whom). • Use the A•B•Q or Top of the Minute Template to record student responses and actions.
Encourage Evidence How are students analyzing their sources of information? What choices do they make?	• Count the number of instances in which students voluntarily cite their sources or ask about evidence from others. • Note the activities in which students have a choice in what, where, how, and with whom they get to accomplish their work.
Extend Thinking Time Describe the pace of the class. How much wait time is offered? Are students given time to reflect?	• Make note of when transitions happen and at what times during the lesson. • Make note of opportunities for students to quietly reflect in writing. • Using your phone's stop watch, calculate the number of seconds between a question being asked and answered. • Describe the pace of the lesson (teacher's voice, movement).

 Available for download at **https://www.inquirypartners.com/**

EXPERIENCE #5

What's the Student Experience?

Although it would be incredibly instructive and eye-opening, most of us cannot get away with going undercover to see what really goes on inside our school's classrooms. However, if you can get the release time and agreement from your colleagues, it is possible to shadow a student and go through the motions of school alongside other students.

Alexis Wiggins, an international school teacher and founder of the Cohort of Educators for Essential Learning (CEEL), was once offered this very experience a few years ago. Her reactions soon went viral and appeared in a *Washington Post* under the compelling title: "Teacher spends two days as a student and is shocked at what she learns." Paraphrasing, Alexis writes:

> *I have made a terrible mistake. I waited fourteen years to do something that I should have done my first year of teaching: shadow a student for a day.*
>
> ### *Key Takeaway #1: Students sit all day, and sitting is exhausting.*
>
> *If I could go back and change my classes now, I would immediately change the following three things:*
>
> 1) *mandatory stretch halfway through the class,*
> 2) *put a Nerf basketball hoop on the back of my door,*
> 3) *build in a hands-on, move-around activity into every single class day.*

What would your Key Takeaways be if you were to shadow a student at your school? What might you change in your classroom following this experience?

There's only one way to find out! Make arrangements to be a student in your school's classrooms (for an hour, half day, or full day). Reflect upon the experience using The Student Experience Template. How would you share your experience with your colleagues?

The Student Experience Template

Key Takeaway #1: _____

If I could go back and change my classes now, I would immediately:

1)

2)

3)

Key Takeaway #2: _____

If I could go back and change my classes now, I would immediately:

1)

2)

3)

Key Takeaway #3: _____

If I could go back and change my classes now, I would immediately:

1)

2)

3)

online resources ⤷ Available for download at **https://www.inquirypartners.com/**

EXPERIENCE #6

What Does All This Tell You?

Let's pull it all together now. Gather your inquiry self-survey, student surveys, peer observation feedback, and student shadow experiences (or whatever you have) in one place. Read through them. Taken together, what do they tell you? Is there a story or a pattern?

Use the following questions to guide your reflection. Share these responses with a partner or group of colleagues. After a couple of months, reassess with new surveys and data. What's changed, and why? If not, why not? How can this reflective process become ritualized in your school?

Pulling It All Together

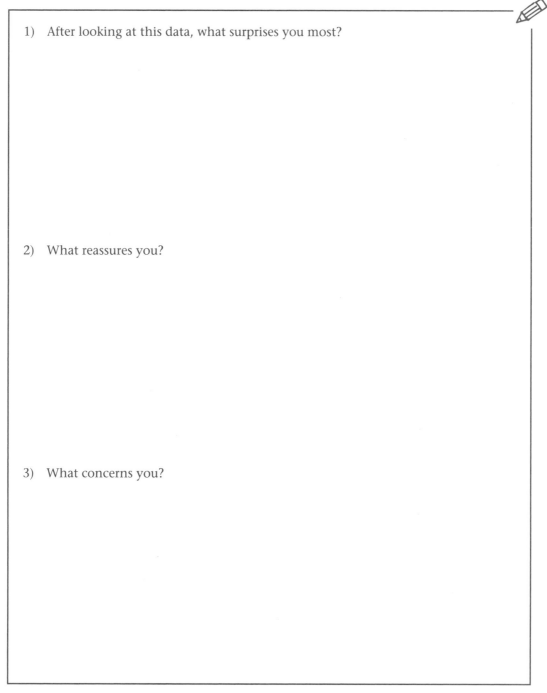

1) After looking at this data, what surprises you most?

2) What reassures you?

3) What concerns you?

(Continued)

(Continued)

4) What additional questions does this raise for you?

5) What are you interested in addressing now? How might you do this?

 Available for download at **https://www.inquirypartners.com/**

WHAT DOES INQUIRY LOOK LIKE?

I've opened thousands of classroom doors to observe classrooms in action on virtually every continent. Most classrooms operate in generally the same way, no matter where I go or when I observe.

The teacher is immediately visible and usually talking. Students are either looking at the teacher or working independently. When I enter, students' heads turn quizzically to me. Could I be the distraction they were hoping for? They have the look of compliance, not curiosity.

Some doors, however, open up to a very different kind of experience. In these classrooms, students are absolutely riveted to their work. They are literally leaning over their desks or workspace. They don't look up when I enter the room. They are talking animatedly with one another, excitedly asking questions and sharing ideas. They have already practiced norms and know the routines. They are not waiting for instructions from their teacher. They understand the purpose of their time together and what's expected of them.

And the teacher? The teacher is often hard to locate at first. They are often crouched around tables with students or sitting quietly taking notes, listening. They speak only to alert the students of how much time is left, where to find supplies or support, or to periodically share their own questions and excitement. Their comments are carefully chosen. The teacher is relaxed. It's the students who are working hard. These are what I call inquiry classrooms.

Make no mistake, inquiry classrooms are painstakingly planned and strategically curated by teachers. The teachers' beliefs and actions create this environment.

HOW DO THEY GET THIS WAY?

Finding the answer to this question defined much of my work over the last couple decades. My methods really varied over the years. I watched inquiry teachers. I collected voice data from their classrooms. I read research. I tried implementing inquiry in my own classroom. Here's what I've discovered:

- *Inquiry requires both a disposition (set of beliefs) and a set of specific actions.*
- *Inquiry cannot be mandated from above. The teacher is one who needs to implement this style of teaching. It will fail unless the teacher believes that students are truly capable of leading their own learning.*
- *There are five essential strategies at play in every inquiry classroom. While these strategies may not seem earth-shattering on the surface, taken together and practiced regularly, they result in radically different kinds of classrooms.*

I call these strategies the Inquiry Five. These five strategies form the structure for the remaining exercises inside this book. The first two strategies are teacher dispositions (those essential beliefs). The other three strategies are behavioral moves that derive from these dispositions.

Narrowing a complex set of beliefs and behaviors into just five strategies is an imperfect science. They do, however, offer the perfect starting point for teachers who are eager to increase, improve, or implement inquiry teaching practices.

The Inquiry Five Strategies

#1. GET PERSONAL

The teacher believes that both she and her students are capable of solving complex problems and worthy of love. The teacher prioritizes relationships above all else in the classroom and finds ways to continually build emotional bonds with the students, between the students, and with the content. The teacher knows that loving and taking good care of oneself is the key to loving and taking good care of others.

#2. STAY CURIOUS

The teacher is willing to strategically step aside and see her students as capable thinkers and, at times, co-teachers. Instead of maintaining a disposition of "all-knowing," the teacher is able to express a sense of shared wonder about the world and model what it means to be curious and always learning.

#3. ASK MORE, TALK LESS

The teacher encourages students to ask questions and seek answers to those questions. The teacher asks students carefully timed, sequenced, and balanced questions. The teacher refrains from spoon-feeding information. She instead offers opportunities for students to struggle and persist in finding answers to their own and others questions.

#4. ENCOURAGE EVIDENCE

The teacher understands that students have an abundance of information at their fingertips. She prioritizes teaching media literacy skills so that students can more confidently identify truth from fiction, understand nuance, and uncover intention.

#5. EXTEND THINKING TIME

Inquiry teachers and students pause and wait for answers, offer opportunities to reflect over longer periods of time, embrace the importance of physically moving around, and welcome silence, even when it's uncomfortable.

EXPERIENCE #7

What Are Your Burning Questions About Inquiry?

Inquiry starts with questions that arise from genuine curiosity, not just parroting the questions you think others want to hear or ticking off the questions you *should* ask. Since inquiry is fueled by real, authentic, *burning* questions, it's important that you have dipped your toe into the inquiry waters long enough to be able to generate some questions of your own (and keep this list going as you move through the experiences in this book). Are you ready?

Set your timer for 10 minutes. Use the following page to scribble down all the burning questions you have about inquiry. What are your concerns? What excites you most about inquiry? What resistance or tension do you feel? Don't stop to judge, discuss, or evaluate your questions. Just let them flow! If you've stopped before 10 minutes have passed, wait and see if any more questions arise (they usually do). Being thoughtfully idle is OK, too.

(PS: Try using this with your students. After introducing a topic, assigning a text or video, give students time to simply pause, think, and generate questions about it first.)

EXPERIENCE #8

Who, When, and How Should You Answer Questions?

Questions come up in every classroom, but they are handled differently in an inquiry setting. One of the starkest differences I see between a traditional classroom and an inquiry classroom comes down to *who, when,* and *how* questions are answered. Record one of your lessons (or ask a colleague to come in) and observe what happens in your own classroom.

Who answers most of the questions? Is it usually you, the teacher; the same two or three students; everyone equally; the textbook; experts?

When are questions answered? Do your students need to answer immediately, or do you allow questions to simmer for a while? How long are you willing to allow students to be "wrong" about something before finding a way to correct them?

How are questions answered? Are they posted and reviewed periodically? Do they come with evidence? Are they definitive or tentative? How do you correct wrong answers?

EXPERIENCE #9

How Can Questions Be Savored?

Do you remember the thrill of Halloween as a child? The best part of the night for me was tearing off my sweaty mask and dumping my fun-size candy out onto the living room floor. I don't know what my sisters and I enjoyed more: eating our candies or sorting them into piles.

Pretend that the questions you (or your group) came up with from Experience #7 are your "question candies." Dump them out together into one big pile. Now, how might you sort them? Which ones are "$100,000 Bars" (special and unique)? Which ones are "Snickers" (dime-a-dozen)? Are there any "full size" (big, dense questions) to admire and savor over time?

First, simply read through what you all have. Are there questions that appear again and again? If so, consolidate. Then, decide what kinds of categories you want to create and go to town!

One way to organize your questions is to place them into just two groups: divergent questions (open-ended) and convergent questions (closed). Which questions might have several answers, and which ones are straight-forward and factual? This activity alone will turn into great discussion and debate if you are working with others (you'll have to get very clear on how you decide to further define these two terms).

After you've finished sorting your questions, choose up to five that you consider to be "priority questions." These are the questions you are most interested in exploring the answers to. Take your priority questions and write them in the space provided. (If you are working as a staff on this, consolidate all priority questions onto large sheets of paper that can be posted publicly.)

Allow your understanding to develop collaboratively and over time. This means that the questions may be unanswered or only partially answered for days, weeks, or months. Allow multiple answers and additional questions to emerge (allow some evolution to take place by keeping extra space open for new, emerging questions). Keep returning to this exercise to complete your answers.

Next to each possible answer (there may be several for each question), cite the various sources consulted (even if it's simply "my own experience" or "I read it in a book with a yellow cover and the word 'inquiry' in the title").

DIVERGENT QUESTIONS (OPEN)	CONVERGENT QUESTIONS (CLOSED)

SAVORING QUESTIONS

PRIORITY QUESTIONS	POSSIBLE ANSWER(S)	SOURCE(S)

 Available for download at **https://www.inquirypartners.com/**

EXPERIENCE #10

What Does Your "Ideal" Class Look Like?

What might you see, hear, and feel when you open the door to *your* ideal classroom? Be as specific as you can. Which of these ideal characteristics do you think are universal to all teachers? Which are the hardest to achieve? Which apply only to your style of teaching? Which do you already see in your own classroom, and which would you like to see more of? Start your lists below. Continue to add to the list as you go through the experiences in this book.

WHAT WE MIGHT *SEE*:

WHAT WE MIGHT *HEAR*:

WHAT WE MIGHT *FEEL*:

BONUS! WHAT WE MIGHT *SMELL* (LET'S AVOID TASTING, SHALL WE?):

CHAPTER

5

STRATEGY #1: GET PERSONAL

"Sometimes a simple, almost insignificant gesture on the part of a teacher can have a profound formative effect on the life of a student."

—Paulo Freire, *Pedagogy of Freedom*

Introduction to Get Personal

In third grade, my PE teacher Ms. G called me "an athlete" in front of the whole class. I remember sitting there with my classmates on the gym mat, my cheeks burning with embarrassment and pride. I didn't see myself in this way at all. I was terrified of dodgeball, flailed in swimming pools, and couldn't properly throw a ball.

But I danced. I also learned to do back handsprings across a grass field. I whipped myself around those cold steel bars at recess so fast my shoes would fly off. Ms. G noticed this. She called me an athlete, and that word became part of my story, a part of my identity. I would do anything for Ms. G to live up to that compliment, too. Gym class went from being my least favorite to most favorite time of the day.

This blip of an experience (a "simple, almost insignificant gesture on the part of a teacher") changed the way I saw myself forever. It fueled my desire to try out new ways to challenge myself athletically: I climbed mountains, I ran distance races, I eventually learned to throw a ball.

Without a strong emotional foundation with and between your students, the incentive to work hard and do well will disappear faster than donuts from the staff lounge. You already know this, but isn't it amazing how quickly we forget to keep stoking the relationship fire? *Your students have to know you, and you them, and they each other in order to create space for authentic inquiry and intellectual risk taking.* The high demands and frenzied pace in schools mean we often cut corners with relationships. We bark orders. We pile on busy work. We fail to make eye contact or smile. We forget to say something nice. We run out of time. Sometimes we even forget to breathe.

How can we remember to be human and happy?

As basic as it sounds, knowing and loving yourself is the first step to developing happy human relationships—and making authentic inquiry possible. The exercises that follow are opportunities to remind yourself of *who you are* so that you can loosen up and communicate your unique fabulousness to your students.

EXPERIENCE #11

WHO ARE YOU?

TEACHER EDITION

My name is _____, but my students call me

_____. I've been teaching for _____ years and

would describe these years as _____ and _____.

My students would probably describe me as _____,

_____ and _____.

My favorite part of the school day is _____

because _____.

My least favorite part of the school day is _____

because _____.

I know I'm a successful teacher when _____

_____.

If I weren't teaching, I'd probably be _____.

After filling the blanks on this page, read it aloud to a colleague and listen to theirs. What did you learn? What questions does it raise for you? What questions does it raise for them? Create your own fill-in-the-blanks to help answer some of those questions.

online resources ⬏ Available for download at **https://www.inquirypartners.com/**

WHO ARE YOU?

STUDENT EDITION

My name is _____, but my friends call me

_____. I've been a student at this school for _____ years and

would describe these years as _____ and _____.

My teachers would probably describe me as _____,

_____and _____.

My favorite part of the school day is _____

because _____.

My least favorite part of the school day is _____

because_____.

I know I'm a successful student when _____.

When I'm not in school, I like to _____

_____.

After filling the blanks on this page, read it aloud to a fellow student or share with a teacher. Listen to theirs. What did you learn? What questions does it raise for you? What questions does it raise for them? Create your own fill-in-the-blanks to help answer some of the questions you have about the person you heard from.

 Available for download at **https://www.inquirypartners.com/**

EXPERIENCE #12

Who Were Your Teachers?

Ms. G made a difference in my life in terms of how I viewed myself athletically. But it was Mr. H who changed the way I viewed myself academically. He was my sixth-grade teacher and my first male teacher. Tall and skinny with a bushy moustache, Mr. H drove a red VW van. He sang funny songs, which we would echo back to him at the tops of our lungs. Mr. H was a gifted storyteller, and his passion in life was opera. Mr. H was determined to share this passion with his class of 11-year-olds every year. Sixth-grade students and *opera?* Yes! It worked because stories work!

Mr. H would choose one of his favorite operas of the season to share with us during the year. He would escort all of us into a tiny amphitheater every Friday afternoon to unspool the opera storyline. We would perch ourselves tightly on the dusty steps theater-style and listen to him, our heads perched on our hands, rapt with attention. It was our favorite time of the week. What makes some teachers so memorable? How do we describe their impact?

At the start of every quarter I ask my new students to make a list of every teacher they've ever had from Kindergarten through the end of high school. This exercise takes about 15 minutes to complete, and they find it both challenging and eye-opening.

Many students will identify the teachers who made a positive impact, but every so often we will hear about the negative ones. And while high school may be fresh in their minds, there are an equal number of memories of early elementary teachers and coaches. Nearly every subject area is represented. The content is rarely, if ever, the reason the teachers were so memorable (case in point, it wasn't about the opera). Some of my students' most impactful teachers were showboats and funny, while others were soft-spoken and awkward. What they all had in common was the ability to emotionally connect with their students.

Who Were Your Teachers?

Make a list of as many of your pre-school through Grade 12 teachers as you can. If you were homeschooled, this will be easy. If you were in a multi-age classroom or attended school in another country, adjust as needed. If you cannot remember a name, simply describe the person. For years where you had several teachers, write all the teachers you can remember from that year.

When you've exhausted your memory, circle the name of just *one* teacher (or coach/instructor) who you feel had the greatest (positive) impact on your life. Use the next page to write a short reflection of or letter to this teacher. What was it about this person that made such an impact? What ideas or strategies have you borrowed from this person for your own teaching practice? If you can locate this teacher, consider mailing this letter to them.

GRADE	TEACHER NAME(S)	COACHES AND OTHER INSTRUCTORS
Pre-school		
Kindergarten		
1st Grade		
2nd Grade		
3rd Grade		
4th Grade		
5th Grade		
6th Grade		
7th Grade		
8th Grade		
9th Grade		
10th Grade		
11th Grade		
12th Grade		

online resources Available for download at **https://www.inquirypartners.com/**

A Thank You Letter to My Teacher

EXPERIENCE #13

What Stories Can You Tell?

One of the reasons inquiry teachers tell lots of stories in the classroom is to deepen emotional connections with their students. Human brains are wired for learning through narratives and stories. Stories help students better understand and remember content. It's a shame there isn't a mandatory course during teacher training on the art of storytelling. But it's never too late to learn!

Storytelling is one of our most ancient and effective teaching practices. Stories don't always need to be lengthy, and they don't necessarily need to follow the Aristotelian Arc to be effective. They can be as simple as a quick anecdote or even a metaphor. At the core, stories just need to be honest or honestly told.

Who are the storytellers in your life? How do they approach their work? Do you consider yourself a good storyteller? Why or why not? How often do you tell stories to your friends, family, and students?

There are two storytellers who have helped me understand the power of storytelling in teaching: Carmen Agra Deedy and Lynda Barry. While their styles differ, both of these women create magic through storytelling.

CARMEN AGRA DEEDY

Carmen was born in Cuba, and her family fled to Decatur, Georgia, as refugees when she was a child. She overcame learning challenges to become a prolific author and gifted storyteller. Listening and watching her speak at a conference in Chicago several years ago was an almost religious experience for me. After she spoke, I met her at a reception. I couldn't help myself; as soon as we made eye contact, I burst out: "I just *love* you!"

Accustomed to fans like me, she just laughed and gave me a hug. Since then, we've shared a meal together, and she's inspired my work even further. As with any talent, Carmen insists that great storytelling takes rigorous practice. While it may appear that she speaks extemporaneously, her stories are actually painstakingly perfected over time. She will work on just one 10-minute oral story for weeks; over and over again. The tone, timing, and words must be perfect.

LYNDA BARRY

Lynda grew up in Seattle, surviving a difficult childhood with the help of a few great teachers. At a young age, Lynda would slip out of her abusive home early in the morning to swing on the monkey bars in the deserted playground of her local elementary school. One day, her teacher, Mrs. LeSane, invited Lynda into the classroom before the other students arrived. She had a little table inside with an abundance of art supplies.

This "simple, almost insignificant" gesture changed Lynda's life. Lynda kept drawing and writing right into and through college. In fact, she went on to become a huge success (comics, books, staged plays, workshops, and more). Today, Lynda is a professor, inspiring young (and old) artists and thinkers. I was fortunate to take a week-long intensive writing class with Lynda many years ago. One of the many creative exercises she had us engage with involved writing through brainstormed lists.

Here's how it works. Make a list of ten units (or topics) you teach throughout the school year (for example, order of operations, *Roll of Thunder, Hear My Cry*, run-on sentences, or global warming). This should take just a few minutes. Then, pick a number 1 through 10 randomly and circle that number. This is what you will write about!

Set a timer for 10 minutes. Let your thoughts, ideas, questions, wonderings, views, and experiences of this topic just spill out of you. When did you first learn this skill or topic? Why is it important to know? What academic questions or mysteries remain about this topic? What makes this unit worth exploring in depth? What's changed about this unit over time (in terms of new research or how people approach it)? What do you like or dislike about teaching this?

Ten Units I Teach

1)   6)

2)   7)

3)   8)

4)   9)

5)   10)

My Reflections on This Unit

online resources Available for download at **https://www.inquirypartners.com/**

EXPERIENCE #14

How Do You Tell a Story That Sticks to the Soul?

Jeff Butler teaches high school math. This is his 23rd year at the same school. He loves his subject but is often challenged by getting his students to appreciate it as much as he does. A black & white poster of the 1968 Olympics Black Panther salute hangs on a classroom wall along with some of his bicycle memorabilia. Aside from these little clues on the wall, students don't really know much about Mr. Butler.

Jeff readily admits to being an "introvert" and hesitates to share too much of his life with his students. As he sees it, his primary job is to get his students through Algebra I, and the clock is ticking. An unconscious belief sits in the back of his mind, too: He never needed much cajoling to focus on math in high school. Why should they? Working with Jeff as an instructional coach is a wonderful challenge. He is open to trying new things but needs guidance and reassurance that revealing more of himself to his students is worth the effort. When I suggested that he add a story to just one lesson he teaches each week, he responded: "I teach Algebra I. How do I tell a story that is relevant to *that*?"

Fair question. We started with the objective of a unit he was about to teach; at the heart of it: inductive reasoning. "What is inductive reasoning, anyway?" I asked him. I prodded him to tell me a story to explain it. Pretend I'm your elderly grandmother. Make it simple; make it stick to my soul.

After thinking for a couple minutes, he began: "It's like you have a bag that you cannot see through, and then you pick out a few objects and, well, maybe the only things you pick out are …" he pauses here and says, "Green apples. Yeah. And so, you assume or infer or induce that it's a bag filled entirely of green apples."

This was it! After creating and practicing this story to make it relate to something honest and true in his own life, Jeff tried it out with his students the next day.

Jeff's large hands form around an invisible apple as he tells the story, growing from one small apple to a bushel of them, his arms opening wide.

He adds some personal notes about walking his dog to the neighbor's apple tree. I watch as students sit up, smile, and ask questions about his dog, where he lives, what he does with the apples he receives. They've never experienced this teacher getting so personal. They love it.

Jeff pauses at the end of his story dramatically. He's enjoying this more than he anticipated.

"Take out the apples and replace them with numbers . . . and there's the math!"

His eyes open wide, and the students laugh. They are enthralled. They haven't seen their teacher so passionate ever. The story makes sense. For the first time, his exit tickets demonstrate 100% comprehension on his stated objective. Jeff receives dozens of high-fives from students on the way out the door.

Your turn! Re-read the units you listed in Experience #13. Pick one topic from this exercise (it can be the same one you wrote about or a new one) and create a classic narrative story using either a storyboard or an arc process. A storyboard visually tells the story frame by frame (like a comic book). The arc is for those who would rather use words than images to plot their story. This process will help you identify the pivotal moments around which you can add the sensory details, dimension, and "juice" to your story.

Then, *tell* the story to a partner (as opposed to *explaining how* you might tell the story), and have that person share their story with you. Help one another refine and polish these stories. Find at least three other people to tell the story to again (and listen to them refine theirs). Tell this story to your students when you arrive at this topic in your curriculum. See how you can improve upon it each time. Check out the Galileo Network for a helpful Storytelling Rubric you (and your students) can use to evaluate and improve your stories.

STORYBOARD TEMPLATE

Intro of setting and character(s)	Rising action (events that build up to the climax)
Rising action, continued	Climax (the "turning point")
Falling action (outcome of the "turning point")	Denouement (how life carries on; the resolution)

 Available for download at **https://www.inquirypartners.com/**

Story Arc Template

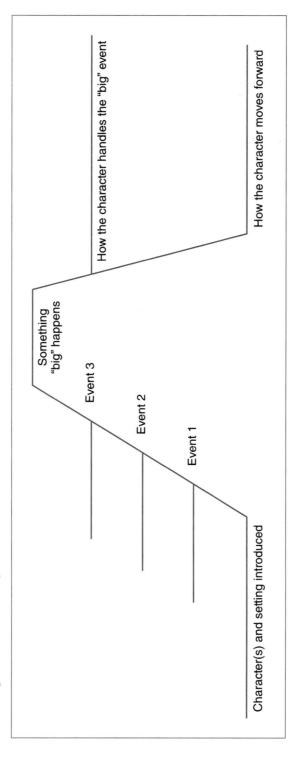

- Character(s) and setting introduced
- Event 1
- Event 2
- Event 3
- Something "big" happens
- How the character handles the "big" event
- How the character moves forward

EXPERIENCE #15

What Does Your Classroom Say About You?

There is an energy inside every classroom, even and perhaps *especially* after the students have left for the day. And a smell. We all know that.

I recently visited a high school government teacher's classroom. Across one wall hung a large bulletin board filled with photos of students, their pets, and their families; a colorful collage of overlapping images. Another wall was covered in college acceptance letters and college pendants. I looked around, marveling at its vibrancy. "Wow, I love your classroom!" I said. I'll never forget her response: "Thanks, but it's not mine. It's my students'."

Your classroom, like your own home, often speaks volumes about you and your relationship with students.

What does your classroom say about you and your role in it? What does it say about your students and their role? Does the environment evoke a sense of calm, excitement, order, or chaos? Are you the king of the castle or is it more democratic?

You and your students spend a significant amount of time inside these spaces called classrooms. While strong relationships and great teaching will always be more important than the physical space, it's worth taking a look at how the space reflects you, your students, and what happens inside. Is it reflecting what you want it to? Does it bring out the best in all of you? If not, why not?

Observations of Someone Else's Classroom

Write everything you see, hear, feel, smell, and sense sitting from one of the student's chairs inside a colleague's classroom. Make sure that your observations are simply that: observations. Avoid commentary, suggestions, or judgements. Make sure you write these notes on a separate piece of paper so that you can hand it to your colleague. Bulleted lists are fine.

Notes From a Visitor to Your Classroom

Read the written observations from your colleague. Are there any surprises? What made you happy to read? What concerned you? What might you do with this information? Write down your reactions and additional questions in the space below.

Observations of Your Own Classroom

Now spend 10 minutes in your own classroom. Try to spend the entire time in one of your student's chairs (maybe switch seats halfway through). Check things out from different perspectives in the room. Start by simply noting what you see, hear, feel, and smell. Are you noticing anything for the first time? How might it feel to be a student in your classroom? How does it feel to be *you* in your classroom? What adjectives would you use to describe your classroom?

EXPERIENCE #16

Why Do You Teach?

My husband and I went through a lengthy adoption process after trying to have a second child. We were struck by how much soul searching we were required to do (and how valuable this process would have been with our first child).

Of course, we do a lot of soul searching when we first became teachers, too. With all the essays, exams, video reflections, and mentor feedback, it was hard not to, right?

But once we have our certification in hand and our teaching career starts rolling, we rarely step back to assess how we're feeling and if we are still as passionate as when we first decided to become a teacher. All too often, years go by without reexamining why we teach.

Inquiry teachers continuously examine the why behind what they do. They share their *why* with students as well. *Why do I teach?* is a question that may change over time. What were all the reasons you went into teaching to begin with? Why are you still teaching now? What's changed between now and then in terms of your *why*? Be as specific and honest as you can in the space provided and share with a colleague.

Why I first went into teaching:

Why I'm still teaching today:

What's changed?

EXPERIENCE #17

What Is the Third Space?

Leaving the classroom to go into administration was a tough transition for me. How was it possible that the *adults* were harder to manage than the students? There was one aspect of administration that I quickly embraced: the ability to physically move around the building freely. I relished the time I could go outside to walk the perimeter of the large campus. My walkie-talkie turned on low and my key ring bouncing heavily on the side of my hip, I would slow my usual fast pace to observe the trees and sky. I'd nod hello to the neighbors taking out their trash or checking their mailbox. I could smell changes in weather and get out of my head for a few precious minutes. This was my "Third Space" or the place where school and life collided for me, in a happy way.

Dr. Leslie Maniotes, her sister Ann Caspari, and their mom Dr. Carol Kuhlthau are among my favorite inquiry researchers and coaches. Their Guided Inquiry book series (Kuhlthau, Maniotes, & Caspari, 2012) is a brilliant mom-and-daughter collaborative effort. One of their chapters focuses on the concept of this Third Space.

The Third Space is where students connect what they are learning to who they are and what they are experiencing outside of the classroom. It blurs the artificial lines between school and life. The Third Space is why students get so excited about dogs wandering into school buildings, standing outside during fire drills, or running into a teacher in the supermarket. These events involve the outside world miraculously meeting the school world. It's a beautiful, dissonant experience. It also forms the basis of experiential learning and inquiry.

Third Space Example

Pick one of your units of study and then use the four corners to list all the connections that you can make between this unit's main objective(s) and the title in each quadrant. Working with a small group of colleagues, pass this Third Space paper around a table and ask others to fill in this space with you. This is a great activity to do with your students, too. (See an example, below.)

UNIT'S MAIN OBJECTIVE(S)

Ask and answer such questions as who, what, where, when, why, and how to demonstrate understanding of key details in a text. (Common Core ELA, Grade 2)

Your Life (Teacher)	**Other Subject Areas/Units**
Invitations to meetings, events, conferences, and parties	ELA: Making sense of stories; why and how authors add these details differently from how journalists approach them
Freeway construction and weather	
Births, deaths, weddings, and other big life events	History: Understanding context and what is happening in other parts of the world at the same time; news and current events
	Science: Tracking issues to understand change over time
Students' Lives ("Third Space")	**The School Community**
Invitations to events and parties, sports, and music practices	School schedules and class agendas
Lunch menus	Large school events like assemblies, drills, parent meetings
Regular after-school events and schedules	Announcements to parents
Sports-related events, games, and articles	Local newspaper articles

Your turn! Pick one of your units of study and then use the four corners to list all the connections you can make between the unit's main objective(s) and the title in each quadrant. Working with a small group of colleagues, pass your paper around, and ask others to add in more ideas.

A note from the authors: While this particular Third Space activity helps you to access Third Space in one moment of time, it's worth remembering that this is an activity to get you thinking about how Third Space can permeate the classroom beyond a single unit.

Third Space Template

UNIT'S MAIN OBJECTIVE(S)

_____

_____

Your Life (Teacher)	Other Subject Areas/Units
Students' Lives ("Third Space")	**The School Community**

Source: Guided Inquiry Design, Kuhlthau, Maniotes and Caspari (2012), ABC-CLIO. Adapted with permission by Kimberly L. Mitchell

 Available for download at **https://www.inquirypartners.com/**

EXPERIENCE #18

Ask Me Anything!

To close this chapter, let's go back to the beginning. We teach who we are, or in the words of Marshall McLuhan, "The medium is the message." The teaching–learning process is inextricably wrapped up in human emotion. Do you feel as though your students don't care about anything you teach? Try talking about yourself! I've never met a student who wasn't insanely curious about their teacher's life. Even my university students want to know more about me and their other kooky professors.

Capitalize on their curiosity to strengthen emotional bonds by answering their questions about you. Offer your students time to write down questions they have about you on strips of paper and place them in a box. After reading through (and selecting only the ones you are comfortable answering), set aside 10 minutes once a week to answer from the Ask Me Anything Box. The element of surprise ("Will she choose my question today?") and intimacy ("I love Rocky Road ice cream, too!") will strengthen emotional bonds between you and the students.

FIGURE 5.1 ■ *It's a Teacher's Life*, David Sipress (1993)

CHAPTER

6

STRATEGY #2: STAY CURIOUS

"Curiosity is the very basis of education, and if you tell me that curiosity killed the cat, I say only the cat died nobly."

—Arnold Edinborough, Canadian author

Introduction to Stay Curious

The lines between teacher and learner are blurred in an inquiry setting. Students learn by teaching. Teachers teach by learning.

What's your disposition as a *learner* in your classroom? What about your content still intrigues you? What about teaching still intrigues you? How do you communicate your own curiosity with your students? How do you share unanswered (or, unsatisfactorily answered) questions with them?

The exercises in this chapter are designed to help you identify where, what, and from whom you are *still* learning, so you can share this disposition of curiosity with your students. This is a significant departure from traditional models of teaching, where the teacher is assumed to have all the answers.

No one likes a Know-It-All.

Besides, you *don't* know it all. No one does. Will your students still respect you if you don't know the answer to everything? Yes! In fact, students find it refreshing to hear their teachers say, "I'm not sure about that. How might we find out?" I'm not saying we don't need to know our content and pedagogy: We do! It's just that there are limits to everyone's knowledge and understanding. These limits are what motivates us to learn more!

For many years, I named this strategy "Maintain Neutrality." Curious teachers react to student conjectures with equanimity rather than judgement. In other words, instead of being the sole arbiter of something being right or wrong, inquiry teachers remain neutral, allowing students themselves to assess the validity or soundness of comments.

However, maintaining neutrality is a *behavior* that stems from a *disposition of* curiosity. There are multiple ways to show that you are open to learning and eager to share the role of teacher in your classroom. The following experiences are designed for you to strengthen your curious disposition.

EXPERIENCE #19

What's Your Expertise?

The purpose of this exercise is to demonstrate how much there is *still* to learn even about something you know a whole lot about. What *do* you know a whole lot about (in or outside of your content area)? Asked another way, if you were to write a nonfiction book about something, what would you write about? Set your timer for 10 minutes and brainstorm in the space below:

Your Nonfiction Book

Read through your list and choose just *one* topic to expand upon. Choose the one that most appeals to you at this moment. Think about all the knowledge, skills, and beliefs that go into being an expert on this topic. Outline the chapters that would make up a book about your topic, including the main question(s) each chapter would explore.

CHAPTER TITLES	THE MAIN QUESTIONS YOU'D ANSWER IN THIS CHAPTER

EXPERIENCE #20

What Still Intrigues You?

Every subject has its controversies, unresolved mysteries, and unknowns. We're finding new planets, watching species quickly disappear from Earth, creating Artificial Intelligence. Schools don't always communicate these exciting and controversial innovations very well. We seem to be stuck in the past, relating what happened rather than kicking in the promise of what *can* happen in the future.

But we can change this. We can remind students that even though they are being asked to remember stuff and read others' research, the world is ripe for contesting and creating.

Jerome Bruner (1986, p. 126), the late cognitive learning psychologist, remembered his fifth-grade teacher in this way:

> I recall a teacher, her name was Miss Orcutt, who made the statement in class, "It is a very puzzling thing not that water turns to ice at 32 degrees F, but that it should change from a liquid into a solid."
>
> She then went on to give us an intuitive account of Brownian movement and of molecules, expressing a sense of wonder that matched, indeed bettered, the sense of wonder I felt at that age (around 10) about everything I turned my mind to . . .
>
> In effect, she was inviting me to extend my world of wonder to encompass hers. She was not just informing me. She was, rather, negotiating the world of wonder and possibility. Molecules, solids, liquids, movement were not facts; they were to be used in pondering and imagining.
>
> Miss Orcutt was the rarity. She was a human event, not a transmission device.

Read through your draft chapter titles from Experience #19. What are the biggest controversies and unresolved mysteries that continue to surround this topic? Write some of them in the space below and share with a partner or group:

Take 10 minutes to explore these questions further online. List all the new ideas and questions that came up for you after conducting this research in the space below.

NEW IDEAS AND QUESTIONS	WEBSITES I CONSULTED

online resources — Available for download at **https://www.inquirypartners.com/**

EXPERIENCE #21

Who Are Your Teachers Today?

Beginner's Mind or "Shoshin" is a Zen Buddhist term that refers to a disposition of openness and a willingness to learn something new (or anew). The true challenge of Beginner's Mind is confronted for example when one is re-learning something, learning from someone one disagrees with, or learning something in a way they find uncomfortable. More than anything, Beginner's Mind requires the learner to set ego aside (the need to be right or know it all) so that the opportunity for new learning can be achieved. Approaching life with Beginner's Mind takes practice.

WHEN ARE *YOU* A STUDENT, AND WHAT KIND OF STUDENT ARE YOU?

Perhaps it's right now. Are you open to learning something new? If not, why not? Earlier in the book, you reflected on the teachers you had growing up. Who are your teachers *today*? They may be formal teachers (a coach or an instructor) or informal ones (your neighbor, child, or even a pet). Brainstorm all the teachers in your life today in the space below:

Reflect on the list of teachers you jotted down. When you are ready, choose three who you feel are having the most impact on your life today. What lessons are you learning from them? In the last row, write something you would like to learn, but haven't yet. Who are your *potential* teacher(s)? Finally, reflect on what you may be learning again or what you've tried, but feel you've failed thus far, to learn.

Your Teachers Today

MY TEACHERS TODAY	THE BIGGEST LESSONS
Something(s) I'd like to learn:	Potential Teachers:

I'm re-learning . . .

I tried, but I feel I failed to learn . . .

online resources Available for download at **https://www.inquirypartners.com/**

EXPERIENCE #22

Are You a Luddite or LinkedIn?

The amount of information readily available to us today can make life easier or induce a panic attack (I've felt both). Smartphones, apps, gaming, coding, social media, virtual reality, augmented reality . . . it's easy to feel overwhelmed. There was a time when my response was to throw up my hands and just call myself "old school." But that's a cop-out.

How can I harp on the importance of having a growth mindset and "doing hard things" with my students if I don't model it myself? I must be willing to at least try. As soon as I gave into learning to be a techie, I realized that I'm actually further along in my understanding than I first thought. In the words of the fabulous tech educator, Alice Keeler: *"The only difference between 'I'm a techie' and 'I'm not a techie' is the willingness to click on stuff and see what happens."*

Easy enough! We can all be techies. My students share a new app with me just about every day. The latest is an alarm clock app that once set, won't turn off unless you've made it out of bed and into the bathroom (proving it with a snapshot of the toilet). Genius!

When someone shows you a new app that you just *have to use*, how do you feel? Write an adjective or two in the box below and share with your colleagues:

I could spend all day exploring apps, but I don't. I stick with my favorites until someone convinces me to try something new. Some have saved me time, challenged my brain, calmed me down, and managed my health. A few I regularly use in my classroom.

If you've been reluctant to jump into the ball pit of apps, it's time! Take off those shoes and jump in. Feel what it's like to be a student today. Understand this world so you can leverage it to support learning and inquiry. That alarm is going off. Don't push snooze any longer!

Start here. Open up your laptop or turn on your smartphone. What's on there that you use both outside and in the classroom? Use this chart to inventory the tech tools (apps or programs) you *currently* use.

I, _____ AM A TECHIE!

APP NAME	USE DAILY	USE OFTEN	RARELY USE

(Continued)

(Continued)

MY FAVORITES	WHY I FIND THEM SO USEFUL

 Available for download at **https://www.inquirypartners.com/**

If you are with a group, post these around the room and take a look at each other's charts. Ask people to share more about their experiences and offer mini-lessons. Lose the apps you don't use and make room for new ones. Keep updating and curating!

EXPERIENCE #23

What Do You Teach?

Is your school's curriculum publicly available, shrouded in secrecy, or just plain nonexistent? Do you have some knowledge of what's happening in your grade level or department, but unaware of the rest of the school? Is it important to know?

I think so. Imagine embarking on a mountain climb where the guides take you to one destination and then leave you there not really knowing what the next leg of the journey will be.

Educational researcher Heidi Hayes Jacobs pioneered a process for addressing this issue called "mapping the curriculum." I remember our school dismantling shelves filled with books no one touched anymore to expose an entire wall dedicated to our map. We taped up posters of what each teacher taught and at which point they taught it in the school year: K–5, September to June. It was a revelation; many revelations, in fact.

For example, specialist teachers (music, art, languages, and PE) discovered new places to synergize their work. We noticed that some students could be studying the rain forest 3 years in a row! And, we weren't introducing any statistics or probability until seventh grade. Whoops. The map made our gaps and overlaps fully visible.

THE DISCUSSIONS THAT FOLLOWED WEREN'T ALWAYS EASY, BUT THEY WERE THE RIGHT ONES TO HAVE.

After some unit "horse trading" and revising, we invited high school teachers in to read our map and offer their feedback. As principal, I was so proud of this curriculum map that I would regularly tour parents into the staff lounge to gaze upon our tapestry of units.

What is really exciting about curriculum mapping is that it doesn't have to take months to complete. In fact, the initial phase of mapping is high level and out-of-the weeds (which is why the time allotted for this experience is limited).

Here's how you can easily start mapping your curriculum. Set a timer for just 30 minutes. On the "Curriculum at-a-Glance," write down the main topics, issues, or questions you teach month-to-month in your school year. The space offered is intentionally small. We don't want you to go overboard with this. If you teach multiple classes, make sure you divide each box to show what you teach in each class. Everyone may approach this differently. That's OK. Go with it.

After 30 minutes, make a copy of your page and tape it to a wall with your colleagues' maps (use a vertical axis for grade level and, eventually, a horizontal axis for months of the school year). Spend another 10 minutes (or more) simply reading and silently absorbing. Then, when everyone is ready, offer Post-Its to write reflections, connections, and questions. Place these directly onto each other's pages. How did others interpret this assignment (did they list topics, questions, non-cognitive skills, standards)? What is the student journey schoolwide? Any overlaps or gaps? How might you express your school's curriculum as a story or an illustration? How might you express or present the school curriculum on a single page? Try it in the space provided.

CURRICULUM AT-A-GLANCE

SEPTEMBER	OCTOBER
NOVEMBER	DECEMBER
JANUARY	FEBRUARY
MARCH	APRIL
MAY	JUNE

 Available for download at **https://www.inquirypartners.com/**

THE STUDENT CURRICULAR JOURNEY AT OUR SCHOOL:

Check Appendix for "Curriculum At-a-Glance" for teachers in the Southern Hemisphere. I gottcha, friends!

EXPERIENCE #24

What Would Your Curriculum of Questions Look Like?

In 1969, Neil Postman and Charles Weingartner wrote a seminal book about education, provocatively titled *Teaching as a Subversive Activity*. The subtitle of their manifesto is galvanizing: *"A no-holds-barred assault on outdated teaching methods—with dramatic and practical proposals on how education can be made relevant to today's world."* The image on my paperback edition is an apple with a lit fuse. I used to think this was a rather bold title until someone reminded me of the time and place in which it was written. The 1960s were some bold times.

Remarkably, this book sat on my shelf for years, untouched. Bombastic title aside, it still seemed like another dry, academic book written by two old white guys. It couldn't possibly be relevant today. I was so wrong. Until and unless you do read it, I've been granted permission to reprint an excerpt from chapter 5, "What's Worth Knowing?":

> Suppose all of the syllabi and curricula and textbooks in the schools disappeared. Suppose all of the standardized tests—city-wide, statewide, and national—were lost. In other words, suppose that the most common material impeding innovation in the schools simply did not exist. Then suppose that you decided to turn this "catastrophe" into an opportunity to increase the relevance of the schools. What would you do?
>
> We have a possibility for you to consider: suppose that you decide to have the entire "curriculum" consist of questions. These questions would have to be worth seeking answers to not only from your point of view but, more importantly, from the point of view of the students. In order to get still closer to reality, add the requirement that the questions must help the students to develop and internalize concepts that will help them to survive in the rapidly changing world of the present and future.

Page 61 of Postman and Weingartner's book is left intentionally blank. It is the call to action. Reflecting on the students you work with, write down *your* curriculum of questions in the space below. Share your curriculum with others and talk about how you might prioritize or incorporate these questions in your classrooms today.

EXPERIENCE #25

What's Your Teaching Approach?

Sprung from the fresh and perpetually creative minds of undergraduate students, this activity has generated some of the most exciting conversations and questions I've heard in my classroom.

Prior to match.com and numerous other online dating apps, there was a popular singles activity called "speed dating." Do you remember this phenomenon? Speed dating was built upon the idea that compatibility can be determined within minutes, maybe even seconds, of meeting someone.

One of the readings I assigned to my class a couple years ago was a 2009 paper on how school systems approach teacher selection and assignment called *The Widget Effect,* published by The New Teacher Project, or TNTP. A small group of students were in charge of leading the class discussion based on that reading.

Student Noah Bonner reflected,

> The two main points that stood out to me were: 1) teachers aren't easily replaceable and 2) the teacher evaluation process is still mostly binary. I came up with the idea of teachers being rotated around to teach different subjects because the article also talked about how some teachers did not always have an undergraduate degree in or know a lot about what they were teaching.

An awesome activity is born, just like that.

Teacher Speed Dating

This activity works well especially with larger groups (25+). Place yourselves into groups of four or five. One person in every group assumes the role of Teacher and will then rotate as Teacher to the other groups throughout the Exercise.

The Teacher's job is to teach a lesson to their small groups in just 10 minutes (the "speed" part of this activity). You will notice that the lessons are not written as objectives. Yes, they are open and broad lesson topics, to allow for multiple interpretations. As you will see, this is precisely what makes this such an interesting experience. Teachers have only 2 minutes to prepare for their 10-minute lesson.

ART: Teach your students how to shade an apple using gray scale.

HEALTH: Teach your students about nutrition and healthy eating.

MATH: Teach your students Algebra.

HISTORY: Teach your students about the Revolutionary War.

SPANISH: Teach your students basic Spanish.

PHYSICS: Teach your students about buoyancy.

WRITING: Teach your students how to write a five-paragraph essay.

Those assigned the role of the Teacher have the toughest job (goes without saying, right?!). After they teach to one group, they are quickly evaluated ("satisfactory" or "unsatisfactory" to drive home the absurdity of the binary evaluation system) and sent on their way to the next group—with a new 10-minute lesson to prep and teach. You can do as many rotations as you'd like. Each group is able to observe the variety of ways something can be approached and taught.

Here was the amazing thing that happened when we tried this lesson in my classroom. Very quickly the personalities and default approaches of each "Teacher" emerge. Some began by asking the students what they already knew about the topic. Others picked up their notebooks and started writing as though it was their chalkboard. Many admitted they didn't know enough about the topic and asked their students (the group members) to help teach.

Try this activity out in a large staff meeting or even with your students (instead of multiple subject areas, you can have people teach multiple objectives within one of your units, for example).

After this experience, have a conversation together. Here are some suggested reflection questions:

TEACHERS:

Did you change your approach with each new "class"? Why or why not?

Which topic/activity was the most challenging and the most comfortable for you? Why?

STUDENTS:

What did teachers do that was the most and least effective?

Did you learn anything new? Explain.

Did your teacher evaluations change over time? If so, how?

How do you react (as a student in this experience) to subject areas you are less familiar or comfortable with?

EXPERIENCE #26

How Do You Respond to Students?

In a *Harvard Business Review* article investigating the art of listening, authors Jack Zenger and Joseph Folkman compare active listening to the role of a trampoline, wherein the trampoline (or listener) gives "energy, acceleration, height, and amplification" to the thoughts of a child.

Similarly, brain development researchers describe one of the most essential methods for shaping the brain's circuitry as "serve and return." Similar to a game of tennis or catch, the use of facial expressions, gestures, and words going back and forth build and strengthen neural connections.

Our expressions, gestures, and especially our words are the currency of teaching. How we receive and respond to student's ideas, comments, and questions determines how many intellectual risks they will take and how they will continue to communicate with us and others.

DO YOUR REACTIONS SERVE AS A TRAMPOLINE FOR YOUR STUDENTS?

Ask a colleague to visit your classroom for at least 30 minutes (or videotape yourself using a lapel mic, especially if you roam around the room). Make note of the students' comments or questions along with your immediate, verbatim responses (or gestures/expressions).

MY RESPONSES TO STUDENTS

STUDENT COMMENT OR QUESTION	TEACHER RESPONSE

 Available for download at **https://www.inquirypartners.com/**

Read and reflect. Which of your responses encourage continued risk taking and deeper thinking (trampoline)? Is it possible that any of these responses inadvertently shut students down? Are your words neutral or judgmental in any way? What impact does this have in your classroom?

STRATEGY #3: ASK MORE, TALK LESS

"It is a fact not easily learned (and almost never in school) that the 'answer' to a great many questions is 'merely' another question."

—Neil Postman and Charles Weingartner (1969)

Introduction to Ask More, Talk Less

Most teachers talk too much. We all know this. In our zeal to cover curriculum, we often *tell* students what is important to know rather than *create opportunities* for them to find out on their own. How do we create opportunities for students to talk, ask questions, and explore?

ASKING MORE AND TALKING LESS
IS A GENERAL RULE FOR ENGAGING
PEOPLE OF ALL AGES AND IN ALL CONTEXTS.

When students talk, they process information and create new ideas. We *think* when we talk! So, if you are doing most of the talking, guess what? *You're* doing most of the thinking, too. You have enough to do already.

Asking great questions is a great way to promote student talk and thinking in the classroom. But again, you're not the only one with great questions. Getting students to ask great questions and pursue answers to their questions is a hallmark of inquiry classrooms.

REMEMBER, IT'S ALL
ABOUT BALANCE AND HARMONY.

This does not mean that students shouldn't also practice listening. Listening is an important skill, too. There is a time and place for listening to instructions, a story, or a short lecture. Students need "grist" (information, experiences) for the "mill" (processing). But students spend proportionally *way more time* listening to their teachers. Students haven't been taught how to listen to *one another*.

In this chapter, you will collect and analyze data from your classroom before engaging in exercises to help you hand over the talking- and question-asking reins to your students. Letting go will feel good!

EXPERIENCE #27

What's *Really* Happening in Your Classroom?

Imagine a classroom packed with 25 ninth graders and their teacher, a three-person camera crew, 15 parents of incoming eighth graders, and the principal. The principal would often guide parents of incoming ninth graders through this room. This was one of the few classrooms in her building that she could "bank on" to be a hit with visitors (and the one she suggested we film).

When the principal opened the classroom door, she knew that the parents would see attentive students. The teacher was passionate about her subject (English literature), and it showed. She recited passages from the book they were studying by heart. She spoke with enthusiasm and energy. The curriculum was aligned with standards. The lesson objective was clearly displayed on the board. The teacher prepared all night for this lesson knowing she'd have a large audience.

For a few minutes, we all held the same space together. We observed the same lesson, listened to the same voices. But we each came to very different conclusions about what we witnessed. My companions, film professionals, gave the class rave reviews. "She really knew what she was doing in there; the students were so well-behaved."

THE TRUTH IS THAT WHAT WE WERE ACTUALLY FILMING WAS A PRIME (AND COMMON) EXAMPLE OF *DIS*ENGAGEMENT.

You see, we watched a single, randomly selected student. The camera had a tight lens trained on this student for 90 minutes (it was a block period, ostensibly to allow for deeper work and project-based learning opportunities). We "dummy mic'd" several students giving the impression that our objective was to film the teacher's interaction with students, offering a "wide-lens" view of the classroom. But really, only one student's mic was operating.

After filming, we calculated the amount of time this student was reading, writing, listening, and speaking academically during the 90-minute period. The results were heart breaking.

While the class appeared to be active and alive, this student sat and listened to the teacher talk for 86 minutes (or appeared to listen; we cannot be sure what was really happening inside his head). He participated only once, to ask a clarifying question (less than 30 seconds), and he read for a total of 3 minutes. He never wrote. He never spoke to another student. According to the students we consulted with, and the teacher herself, this was a typical class, and the student we filmed is considered "regularly engaged."

The teacher had spent the prior evening re-reading the assigned book chapters and preparing for a discussion. But the discussion was really only between herself and five students. The remaining 20 students were passive listeners, including the student we filmed. Those who did participate were only marginally active and engaged. They responded to the teacher's questions rather than asking their own. They weren't pressed to back up their claims with evidence or take on a different perspective. No one was asked to create something new.

WHAT HAPPENED IN THAT CLASSROOM THAT ALMOST EVERYONE MISSED?

Taken together, it looked lively and engaging. But a closer look, a tighter frame, revealed something very different. The students were compliant, not curious. They knew exactly how to "do school," but it was a classic example of how learning gets lost.

Top of the Minute Template

How much time are your students reading, writing, speaking, and listening academically? Ask a colleague to choose one student *randomly and anonymously* observe this student for at least 20 consecutive minutes. At the top of every minute, the observer should make a note of what they see this student doing (reading, writing, listening, or speaking).

MINUTE	READING	WRITING	LISTENING	SPEAKING
1				
2				
3				
4				
5				
6				
7				
8				
9				
10				
11				
12				
13				
14				
15				
16				
17				
18				
19				
20				
TOTALS:				
PERCENTAGES:				

 Available for download at **https://www.inquirypartners.com/**

Top of The Minute Reflection

In what way(s) do these data surprise you?

Do you think this represents a typical class day? Explain why or why not.

Where are the totals leaning? Does this please or concern you; why or why not?

Is the observed student an "outlier," or does this student generally represent the norm in class? Explain.

EXPERIENCE #28

Who Is Hiding in Plain Sight?

It's easy to sweep the classroom and feel as though everyone is participating fairly equally. But this is how many students can hide, especially in an active, inquiry classroom.

It's not always obvious which students answer only questions directly given, or who is asking their own questions and listening carefully to others' by building upon their ideas.

The ABQ is a great tool to assess student engagement with a wider lens on your students and their interactions. Who in your classroom is hiding (not participating or not *fully* participating) in plain sight?

Before the class begins, sketch out the seating chart on a blank piece of paper (write students names inside each "desk" or box in advance, if you have time). Ask a colleague to come in and record the interactions during a group-based discussion period using your seating chart.

At the end of the observation, it should look something like this:

FIGURE 7.1 ■ An Example of the ABQ After Observing a 50-Minute Class

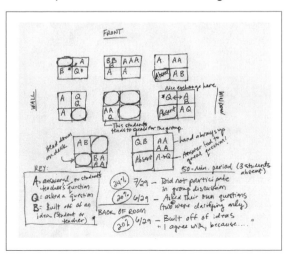

You can also assign students to take on this role within small discussion groups. There are many ways to track conversation (check out Equity Maps, a discussion tracker you can use on your iPad). Here are a couple ways my students tracked their small group conversations (stopping halfway through to share their observations with the group).

FIGURES 7.2 AND 7.3 ■ Conversation-mapping is another way to understand how student discussions are unfolding.

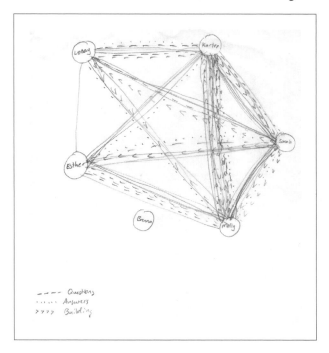

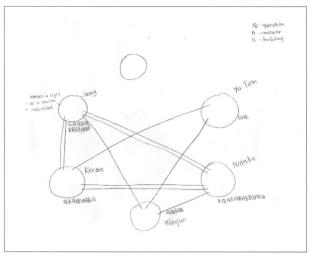

The ABQ Template

Notate every time a student speaks using the following shorthand:

A = Answer (the student answers a question from the teacher or another student)

B = Build (the student builds upon another student's idea)

Q = Question (the student asks a question either of the teacher or another student)

Number of Students: _____   **Minutes observed:** _____

Participants: _____%   **Non-participants:** _____%

Question-askers: _____%   **Question-answerers:** _____%

Builders: _____%

online resources Available for download at **https://www.inquirypartners.com/**

EXPERIENCE #29

What Questions Are You Asking?

Questions aren't all created equally. Some questions can provoke deeper thinking and challenge students to think in creative, new ways. Some merely confirm ideas. Other questions can stop conversations cold.

HOW MANY AND WHAT KINDS OF QUESTIONS DO YOU ASK YOUR STUDENTS DURING A TYPICAL LESSON?

Record yourself during a class period (this can be video or audio via your smartphone or an app, such as the Earshot app). After class, listen and write in the first column all the questions you asked during that period. Then, categorize these questions into groups (see examples below) using the Questions Template.

Factual: Generally, has only one answer
What year was Shakespeare born?

Probing: Invites students to think more deeply about something
Why do you think that?

Clarifying: Asks students to rephrase something for clarity
Are you saying the answer couldn't be twelve?

Confirming: Requires only a yes or no answer
Do you all have your notebooks out?

Rhetorical: Thinking out loud; doesn't require an answer
Can you believe that?

Meta: Exploring the inquiry process itself
Why might this be important for us to ask?

For the purposes of this exercise, simply observe and share your patterns with others. What types of questions are you asking the most, and the least? At which points during the lesson are you asking certain questions? What does the sequencing of your questions reveal to you? Which students do you tend to call on? Which questions and responses do you think led to greater student understanding or creative thinking? Which questions or comments may have unintentionally shut down student thinking and engagement?

To dig into current research on what questions to ask and in what order, I recommend reading Robert Marzano and Julia Simms' *Questioning Sequences in the Classroom* (2014) and Eric Francis' *"Now That's a Good Question!"* (2016).

QUESTIONS TEMPLATE

VERBATIM QUESTIONS	QUESTION TYPE

(Continued)

VERBATIM QUESTIONS	QUESTION TYPE

EXPERIENCE #30

How Do You Teach With Your Mouth Shut?

This title is borrowed from an obscure but important book called *Teaching with Your Mouth Shut* (2000) by the late Evergreen College professor, Dr. Donald Finkel. I learned about this book from a neighbor who took Dr. Finkel's course as a college student. Not long after learning about Dr. Finkel, I met his son who has carried on his father's legacy through an inquiry-based math organization called Math for Love. I'm quite sure the inquiry gods were determined to bring *Teaching with Your Mouth Shut* and these incredible educators into my life. I am grateful.

Dr. Finkel was a pioneer in changing the nature of the college professor's teaching style. He was a passionate teacher who wrestled with questions including, "How do we get students to do more of the talking, question asking, thinking, and creating? How do we, as teachers, step back and stop talking so much? How do we make good on the idea that teaching isn't telling?"

Engaging students at higher levels involves talking less and asking more. It's as simple and complex as that. And it's also easier said than done, especially given the way we've been taught for generations. The first step is building awareness on how much we are telling or "teaching with our mouth open."

Talk Time Pie Chart

When I started working with teachers and schools on implementing inquiry, I found myself noticing and then recording teacher talk time. I would typically use a stop watch to track seconds; stopping and starting over and over again. At the same time, Fitbits were all the rage. This gave me an idea: If I could track my steps, couldn't I track my talk time, too?

It turns out that anything is possible, given time and creative energy. Thanks to the tenacity of my colleague, Amy Satin Spinelli and a team of developers, we created an app for teachers who want to track not only their talk time, but their wait time and questions as well. It's called the Earshot app. So, if you are looking for an easier way to get these data, check it out.

There is no agreement on the "optimal" ratio of talk time between teachers and students. It really depends on the context. That said, too much talking, especially over time, is an indication that the teacher is shouldering too much of the cognitive heavy lifting. Talking is a creative experience and should be a big part of the *students'* experience. Don't take this away from them!

Record yourself during one class period (an hour is usually adequate to collect enough data to see some patterns). If there are small group discussions happening, simply join (or record) one group during the conversation. Then, listen to your audio only. Try not to be judgmental as you listen; simply notice and total of the number of minutes you speak versus the number of minutes your students speak. How much silence is left for just thinking? It's often helpful to illustrate the data using a simple pie chart with colors, so you can really see the balance visually.

Talk Time Pie Chart

Total minutes recorded: _____.

I spoke a total of _____ minutes (red).

Students spoke a total of _____ minutes (blue).

The classroom was silent for _____ minutes (yellow).

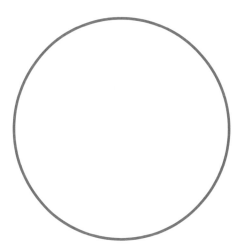

online resources | Available for download at **https://www.inquirypartners.com/**

What do you notice? Was this a typical class period? What made it different? What do *you* think is the ideal amount of teacher v. student talk time for your classroom? Does the subject (or grade level or where you are in the unit) make a difference? Why or why not? How do you come to this conclusion?

If you're comfortable, compare your pie chart with others in your school. As a school, you might post them anonymously up on a wall. What is the schoolwide proportion of teacher and student talk time? Re-post new pie charts on a month-to-month basis to observe any changes over time. Do the silent moments offer students enough thinking time throughout the day? Again, there is no hard, fast rule to this. Have a conversation together as a staff and see what you come up with. Write your reflections to these questions in the space below:

WHO'S TALKING?

MY CLASSROOM	SCHOOLWIDE

EXPERIENCE #31

How Do You Get Students to Listen to One Another?

Who is considered "the knowledge authority" in your classroom? Are students seen as capable inquirers, investigators, and distributors of knowledge? How can you prepare students to listen to one another and hold them accountable to honoring one another as valid sources of information? Read through this short transcript of a high school U.S. government class. There were 26 students in class on this day. Underline or highlight places where the teacher helps guide students to interact with and listen to one another, and not just the teacher.

Teacher: So, how does bureaucracy influence the political agenda in politics?

Student A: Alright so, the bureaucracy was like, we were saying that um, all those, agencies, yeah, that are to help the public, and so I think that teachers' groups and bureaucracy would be connected to what um, what he said yesterday like, the iron triangle?

Teacher: Okay, great, so (student A) ask that question out loud, please.

Student A: How do SCOTUS (Supreme Court of the United States) and the inferior courts influence the political agenda?

Teacher: Say it to the room.

Student A: I don't understand how the SCOTUS and inferior courts influence political agenda.

Teacher: Let's talk about it at our tables really fast.

Students discuss with each other at their tables [1 minute].

Teacher: So, does anyone want to try this? How does the SCOTUS and inferior courts influence political agenda?

Student B: Okay, so, like the video we watched yesterday about the Second Amendment and how it should be, if it should be amended or you know, if it's constitutional to leave out some of these guns from our country, it had go into the court, and if it got appealed, it would go to the Supreme Court eventually . . . the Supreme Court would be in there, and the inferior courts are part of that also and that's also how interest groups get in there.

Teacher: Okay.

Student C: Oh, I can't, I can't . . .

Teacher: Go on . . .

Student C: OK, well. So, I was thinking like, they're like, presidents so if they determine something, then it's probably right for America and it's constitutional so like, if Congress sees an issue that's determined in a court case, they could be like, "Oh, that should be our priority" because the courts think it's constitutional.

Teacher: Alright. I feel like you talked to me when you said that. Can you say that one more time, but say it to the room, please?

Student C: So, I said the SCOTUS (unheard) political agenda by their presidents. Like, if the case is brought to them, and they rule that it's constitutional, then that means Congress and the president would be like, "oh this is constitutional so we should put this at the top of our list" because it's important.

[4 seconds of silence]

Teacher: Can somebody paraphrase what she said?

Student D: So basically, SCOTUS, they decide what's most important, and they put it at the top of the list because they belong to the Constitution and they interpret the Constitution, so . . . yeah.

Teacher notices a hand up.

Student E: Okay, so. Remember how we said that the Supreme Court doesn't really have to do anything about the public because of how Supreme Court you know, stays in court forever. Is that . . . (student trails off and stops talking, looking for the teacher)

Teacher: I want you to talk to the room and not me, so I moved behind you. So yeah, go ahead.

Student E: . . . Is that maybe why she said she shouldn't say it on camera?

Teacher: What do you think? (looking around the room)

Student F: Could it be that like, the media is like, it's only for people to like, get to know her like, ideology about stuff?

Teacher: Well, let's go back to (student E's) question so, say it again.

Student E: Is the reason she said that because she's not from the Supreme Court, so she doesn't have her, um, position as judge or whatever she was?

Teacher: Why do you think she's nervous about saying that on camera?

Student G: Because Obama was running that year, wasn't he?

Teacher: A couple years later, but go ahead.

Student G: Well then, she knew she wanted to be a judge, the supreme judge, and so she didn't want to say anything to like, anything else that would affect her after.

Student H: Yeah, because it's like, with media, they always try to find a way to like, manipulate you. So, it's like, if you say one thing, they'll flip your words around and make it sound worse than, like, you really intended it to be.

What questions does this transcript raise for you?

EXPERIENCE #32

How Do You Get Students to Talk Together?

Traditional classrooms look like a tennis lesson; the teacher lobs a question over the net and a student hits it back. If the ball (question) is successfully returned to the teacher, it is either quickly hit back to the same student or praised. A new question is lobbed by the teacher (other students are waiting).

An inquiry classroom resembles a soccer game. Brazilian soccer player Pele reputedly called soccer *o jogo bonito* or "the beautiful game." This is how it feels to be in a classroom where students are leading their own discussions: *beautiful!* In an inquiry classroom, the teacher is just another player on the field or the referee (although students can play this role as well). A question coming from the teacher or a student is either strategically passed to another student who then may look around the room and pass it on. Or, another student just gracefully receives it. The ball goes back and forth among students without any one person dominating.

Norwegian inquiry education researchers, Helle Alrø and Marit Johnsen-Høines (2017), expand on this idea by suggesting that inquiry doesn't always require posing questions at all. In their research, they explore other ways of communicating in an inquiry classroom, for example fostering student discussions characterized by "equality, unpredictability and risk taking." Teachers who are constantly interjecting questions can often interrupt the flow of thinking. Students need freedom to speak up, take turns without raising their hand, and move the discussion in new directions unhindered. These are skills they will use throughout their lives, at the dinner table, the boardroom, the lab, or the community caucus.

A great example of "the beautiful game" played in the classroom context comes from J. W. Lindfors' book, *Children's Inquiry* (1999), where she transcribes the following early elementary class discussion:

Text No. 11: A Science Talk

Tom: Air takes up, um, space, but does voice?

Lester: I think it sort of does because like, it's like air, and voice is like air so it's . . .

Ellen: Sort of . . .

Tom: Like if you, like if she can blow up a balloon up with your, with your, um, breath, it, um, must take up, it must be matter, sort of.

Eli: It must be matter sort of, 'cause . . .

Tom: Like if you blow up a balloon, like it takes matter.

Ellen: I think it might be matter because, um, when you talk, you breathe out and you breathe in, so . . .

Tom: Yeah, but if you breathe, um, talking, um, you can, you still, um, when some people talk, um, they're like talking a lot, they have to like, get their breath.

Tom: If voice is, um, matter, um, is like, would we be getting squished right now, if it's like, taking up room?

Lester: No, it wouldn't exactly be getting like squished.

Ellen: Because air's taking up space, and it's not squeezing us.

Zach: And it takes up more space than we do.

Teacher: Could you say your question again, Tom?

Zack: How could it not really like . . .

Tim: If, if . . .

Zach: Squeeze us . . .

Tom: If voice is matter . . .

Zach: to death?

Tom: Why isn't it, like, smooshing us against the walls?

Michael: Because air is matter, but when there's like, like take a big wind, for instance. When hurricanes or tornadoes come along, they take up a lot of air, and space, and they are air. But it's just a big quantity of air . . .

Lester: Sometimes the voice waves are, are not as hard as winds can be. Voices waves aren't.

Ian: But how can you tell voice is matter if . . . It seems like air *doesn't* take up space, but it actually *does*. So, so you can't, you can't exactly tell with air where, like, where it is. There's not like, one piece of air going in a different place. That's not the same as with voice. So, it doesn't seem like it would take up room. It's not like every day you see a chunk of air floating around in the sky.

Ellen: Not if it's really cold, and you're breathing, and it gets really cold.

[Sounds of many children breathing in and out]

Ian: Yeah, so. You don't see a chunk of voice flying around if someone says something. It's not like you see these words coming up in a chunk of voice flying up into the air [pointing into the air] "Ohhhh, there's your voice."

Eli: Air can sorta talk. Because when, if, if it's blowing really hard, you can make a noise.

Lester: Voice like, like your voice is the sound.

Ian: Um, I want to, um, add something to Ellen's, but I'm kind of protesting it. But air, air and voice, I don't think they're the same thing. 'Cause if, if voice was air, why wouldn't you just be breathing it instead of talking with it, using it to talk?

Michael: We didn't say they were the same, we just said they were kinda similar.

Teacher: Ian, can you ask that question again because some people have, who've said air is like voice 'cause you breathe out, might want to respond to that. So, Ian, will you ask that again?

Ian: Yeah, yeah, I don't, I don't think voice and air would be the same thing . . . 'Cause it doesn't seem like they're the same thing. Voice, you talk with it, and air, you breathe. So, if they were the same thing, if they were just air, you might not talk 'cause you wouldn't have any voice.

[Later . . .]

Zach: I think voice is matter because like, when you talk, you can feel something like hot on your hand. If you put your hand near your mouth and if you don't talk, you don't have something hot on your hand.

Ian: I just tried that experiment and what I found out, see, I said, "I can." And I found out that when I . . . that hot stuff that I felt on my hand is just breath. I was just breathing.

Eli: But Zach, if that is true, then why can't we really see it happening? Why can't we really see it happening?

Michael: I don't know. It's like air, you can't see air happen.

Zach: You can see it on frosty days.

Michael: Yeah, you can. You see your breath. And your breath is air.

Nate: Well, if you didn't have those tubes in your body, you couldn't speak . . . if you were trying to speak, you would try to speak you'd say nothing. You were saying air.

After reading through the "Text No. 11: A Science Talk" transcript, reflect on and answer the questions below:

Who is doing the talking?

Describe the ways in which students are talking with one another.

What role does the teacher play?

What do students seem to be learning in this discussion?

What would you do next if you were the teacher in this classroom?

EXPERIENCE #33

What Are Socratic Seminars, Harkness, and Spider Web Discussions?

It's time to demystify some terms. Socratic Seminars, Harkness Discussions, and Spider Web Discussions are three terrific methods that inquiry teachers use on a regular basis, in every kind of grade level and subject area, to get students practicing their thinking, listening, communication, and analytical skills together.

Curious? Good! In a group of three, divvy up these terms (jigsaw). Each of you should spend approximately 20 minutes learning as much as you can about each method. As you share, use the Venn diagram that follows to indicate what makes each method similar and unique. Share your experiences with these discussion methods. Invite colleagues into your classroom to watch it in action. Attend others' classes to see how they organize them.

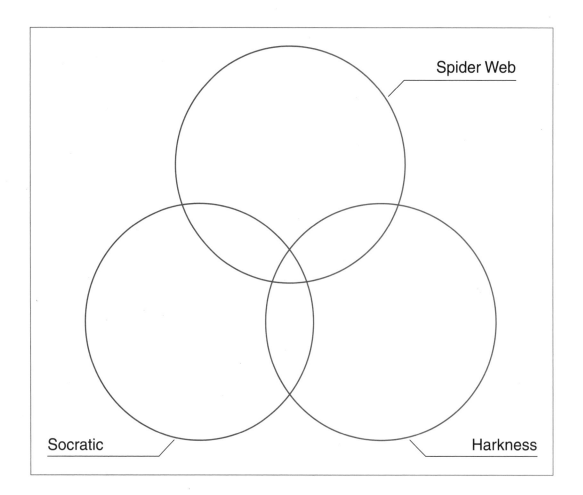

EXPERIENCE #34

Which Questions Work Best in Inquiry Classrooms?

Questions are one of the major energy sources inside inquiry classrooms. Certain questions invite deep critical thinking, regardless of the content or grade level. They are also perfect for laminating onto students' desks, especially as students begin to lead discussions on their own.

Ask a student or colleague to make a check mark next to the questions you ask during a lesson. Which ones seem to be your favorites, and which ones do you want to ask more often? Add more in the spaces below.

GREAT INQUIRY QUESTIONS

Tell me more . . .	How did you make that conclusion?
What do you think?	How did you get that result?
How do you know?	Why?
Can you summarize what _____ just said?	Who can add to that?
Can you put that in your own words?	What are some other possibilities?
What do you all think about that?	Where do those ideas come from?
Do you all agree with _____?	Is _____ correct? How do you know?
Whadya reckon? (Australia)	Add your own.

 Available for download at **https://www.inquirypartners.com/**

STRATEGY #4:
ENCOURAGE EVIDENCE

"When we're not comfortable with math, we don't question the authority of numbers."

—Dan Finkel (2016)

Introduction to Encourage Evidence

The Pacific Northwest tree octopus was a big part of our lives when our son, Van, was in fourth grade. The cephalopod lives in the Olympic National Forest, close to our home. Van spent hours poring over various websites to gather information about how to protect these eight-legged, color-changing, land-lubing creatures. You see, the Pacific Northwest tree octopus is an endangered species.

THEY ARE ALSO A HOAX.

Van's teachers were trying to make a point: You cannot trust everything you read online. It was an ingenious project and a great way to introduce the importance of developing media literacy skills.

The sum of all human knowledge rests literally in the palms of our hands today. Smartphones and the data stored within them have asserted themselves into our lives within a single generation. Teaching is no longer about knowledge transfer, but about making sense of the knowledge that is already available.

INQUIRY WAS PRACTICALLY DESIGNED
FOR THE KNOWLEDGE ECONOMY
AND TECHNOLOGICAL REVOLUTION!

How do we help students (and ourselves) understand the power of bias, perspective, research methodology, memory, context, and time when evaluating sources of information? In this chapter, you will learn more about your own information sources. You will explore how to help students draw back the heavy curtains on the internet to see where their information comes from and how to be savvy, confident consumers of information.

EXPERIENCE #35

What's the Most Important Question to Ask?

When was the last time you challenged someone on the veracity of their information? I'll admit, I don't do it often enough. It can feel impolite and rude. I don't want someone to think I don't trust them.

And yet, asking and answering the question "How do you know that?" should become routine in this age of advanced technology and abundant information. It should become common to hear in our classrooms, for certain.

CITING SOURCES SHOULD BE A MATTER OF COURSE, LIKE SAYING "PLEASE" AND "THANK YOU."

There is one question bouncing around every inquiry classroom, asked by teachers and students alike: *How do you know that?* When you begin asking this question, you will notice that most students will tend to cite personal experiences. Our own personal experiences give veracity to most of our claims. But our experiences are not always generalizable.

STUDENTS SHOULD BE ENCOURAGED TO ASK "HOW DO YOU KNOW THAT?" OF *YOU*, TOO.

Traditional teaching positions the teacher as the authority. I don't remember ever hearing a student ask a teacher to back up their claims or ask why they assigned a specific text. We can be proactive as teachers and back up our own claims, explicitly share the sources from which we present new material, and explain why we chose the resources we do.

HOW DO WE NORMALIZE ASKING THE QUESTION, "HOW DO YOU KNOW THAT?"

Assign one student in your class to ask, "How do you know that?" throughout a class period or day. Of course, you'll need to set some commonsense ground rules beforehand; asking this question should be done judiciously and with care (and the right tone of voice). You can debrief at the end of the day, discussing why the student asked the question when she did, and how other students felt being asked by her.

As an alternative to asking this question verbally (which can interrupt the flow of a discussion), the designated student(s) can also simply hold up the question on a card or piece of paper (see Figure 8.1) from wherever they are seated or standing.

Make sure you process together how it went at the end of a lesson (or staff meeting). How did it feel to be asked to back up a claim or to watch others do it during the discussion? Was it instructive or disruptive? Did it put people too far out of their comfort zones, or was it OK? Is it worth the time it takes to clarify sources? Reflect on these questions and share.

FIGURE 8.1 ■ Use this to signal the need for evidence or a source citation during discussions.

EXPERIENCE #36

How Do You Get Students to Back Up Their Claims?

When I conducted research on orca whales as a fifth grader in the 1970s, I had three library textbooks of varying quality and ancient publication dates at my disposal. If my parents gave me permission to make a long-distance call, I might be able to talk to a research scientist. Maybe. Thinking back on these research methods astonishes me. It feels like the dark ages compared to what we have available today.

ANSWERS TO JUST ABOUT ANY QUESTION TODAY REST LITERALLY IN THE PALMS OF OUR AND OUR CHILDREN'S HANDS.

In an inquiry-based classroom, information is still important. However, the ways in which that information is shared, analyzed, integrated, and used is very, very different. Rather than determining how to present as much information as possible to students in the short time allotted, inquiry takes its time and, as a result, stays with students well after the school year is over.

What happens when we find vastly different answers to the same question? How do we evaluate our sources? Some questions are too broad and ambiguous to be answered by a quick search. The internet curates for us in a biased fashion.

On your own, read through the statements below and decide if you agree, disagree, or are unsure about each statement. Write down your evidence or reasons for agreeing, disagreeing, or being unsure, and then share with a partner or group. After discussing each statement together, set a timer for 10 minutes and choose *one* statement or claim to dig into more deeply. What did your 10-minute research tell you? Did it change anything? What additional questions did it raise for you?

BACK UP THESE CLAIMS

STATEMENT OR CLAIM	AGREE, DISAGREE, UNSURE	WHAT IS YOUR EVIDENCE?	AFTER A 10-MINUTE RESEARCH . . .
Eating too much candy will give you a stomachache.	Agree.	Personal experience; Halloween 1976.	Still agree. Dr. Mercola (licensed physician and surgeon; author) confirms sugar to be toxic, addictive, and even deadly!

Additional Questions:

What is the website used to find this information? Who is Dr. Mercola? What is her specialization? Who funds her research? When was this published? What is meant by "addictive"? Is there conflicting research?

There is too much testing in U.S. public education today.			

Additional Questions:

Half of all new teachers in the United States quit the profession within their first 5 years.			

Additional Questions:

There are 195 countries in the world.			

Additional Questions:

Try this exercise with your own students using statements relevant to your content. Try out a range of closed statements (factual, or with an agreed-upon "right" answer) and open statements (opinion-based, or unsettled research topics). What types of evidence do your students tend to cite in each case? You can allow more time to research and suggest they consult not only the internet, but also books and subject matter experts.

BACK UP THESE CLAIMS TEMPLATE

STATEMENT OR CLAIM	AGREE, DISAGREE, UNSURE	WHAT IS YOUR EVIDENCE?	AFTER A 10-MINUTE RESEARCH . . .

Additional Questions:

Additional Questions:

Additional Questions:

Additional Questions:

online resources — Available for download at **https://www.inquirypartners.com/**

EXPERIENCE #37

How Do You Teach "Crap Detection"?

"One way of looking at the history of the human group is that it has been a continuing struggle against the veneration of 'crap.' Our intellectual history is a chronicle of the anguish and suffering of men who tried to help their contemporaries see that some part of the fondest beliefs were misconceptions, faulty assumptions, superstitions, and even outright lies."

—Postman and Weingartner (1969, p. 3)

Detecting credible, valid sources of information has never been more important than it is today. It comes as no surprise that some of the best ways of detecting crap (yes, that's the academic term) comes from library science specialists. Molly Beestrum and Kenneth Orenic, librarians at Dominican University, created the CRAP Test to help students evaluate websites they use for research purposes. There are four areas they suggest attending to: Currency, Reliability, Authority, and Purpose or Point of View (CRAP is the acronym). So clever! Try it out using one of the websites you chose from the "Back Up Your Claims" Exercise.

Currency

- How recent is the information?
- How recently has the website been updated?
- Is it current enough for your topic?

Reliability

- What kind of information is included in the resource?
- Is content of the resource primarily opinion? Is it balanced?
- Does the creator provide references or sources for data or quotations?

Authority

- Who is the creator or author?
- What are the credentials? Can you find any information about the author's background?
- Who is the published or sponsor?
- Are they reputable?
- What is the publisher's interest (if any) in this information?
- Are there advertisements on the website? If so, are they cleared marked?

Purpose/Point of View

- Is this fact or opinion?
- Does the author list sources or cite references?
- Is it biased? Does the author seem to be trying to push an agenda or particular side?
- Is the creator/author trying to sell you something? If so, is it clearly stated?

Source: Molly Beestrum and Kenneth Orenic

THE CRAP TEST TEMPLATE

Currency	Reliability
Authority	**Purpose/Point of View**

Source: Molly Beestrum and Kenneth Orenic

 Available for download at **https://www.inquirypartners.com/**

EXPERIENCE #38

How Do We Provoke Healthy Debates?

Provocative statements are a great way to get people fired up and insistent on hearing others cite their sources. Choose a provocative statement (sweeping generalizations or controversial beliefs; see examples below) or an image (political cartoons and memes work well).

Try this first with your colleagues. Individually reflect on the statements below and mark an "X" on the continuum of 0 (absolutely not true) to 10 (unequivocally true). You will need to resist the urge to clarify and qualify these statements. Try not to overthink it. The purpose of the exercise is to have a discussion and understand how we back up our claims. This should take no more than 5 minutes to complete (otherwise, you're overthinking it)! Then, discuss and debate each statement in small groups. No need to go in any particular order or come to any consensus.

1 Schools should declare a moratorium on all standardized tests.

0 _____ 10

2 War is inevitable.

0 _____ 10

3 Mosquitos are the most dangerous animal on the planet.

0 _____ 10

4 Parents today are overprotective.

0 _____ 10

5 We should focus on teaching skills, not knowledge, in the 21st century.

0 _____ 10

Did you or anyone change their mind after the discussion? Explain.

PROVOCATIVE STATEMENTS TEMPLATE

Come up with some more provocative statements that relate to the big ideas of a unit you teach. At the beginning of the unit, distribute to students and use as a jumping-off point for a class discussion. Re-administer the statements at the end of the unit and ask students to reflect on how their responses have changed.

Reflect on the statements below and mark an "X" on the continuum of 0 (absolutely not true yet) to 10 (unequivocally true).

1 _____

0 _____ 10

2 _____

0 _____ 10

3 _____

0 _____ 10

4 _____

0 _____ 10

5 _____

0 _____ 10

EXPERIENCE #39

How Can You Practice the Evidence-Seeking Process?

Kira came to my education class while enrolled as a Ph.D. student in physics. Observant, curious, and thoughtful, she inspired me to think more deeply about my own teaching. Within time, Kira went on to teach an Introduction to Physics summer course for underrepresented and first-generation college students.

Kira poured herself into creating an inquiry-based classroom, discovering and refining one activity in particular that simulated the scientific inquiry process in a profound, yet straightforward way. The idea comes from many sources, including the National Institutes of Health (*Doing Science: The Process of Scientific Inquiry*). We call it "Kira's Cube."

Kira's Cube

This is a wonderful activity to implement on the first day of *any* class (not just science), as it simulates the inquiry process in a way that naturally piques interest, requires students to ask questions, and invites them to revise initial thinking based on new data. It also gets students' creative juices flowing and encourages playful group problem solving.

The version of the cube provided on page 144 would work well for older students (middle school and up). For younger students, we've provided a simpler cube (see page 145) with the cube faces holding the numbers 1 through 6, and opposite sides having the same color shade.

IN ADVANCE:

Fold up the cubes. Hide the answer (the "Francene" or "6" side) by covering it with the question mark. Distribute one cube per group of three to four students and ask one person in each group to record everything. Then, lead the groups through the following staged activities (budget about 5 minutes for each stage).

STEP 1: OBSERVATION PHASE

"Pass the cube around to one another and simply make observations about what you see. Gather as many factual pieces of information as possible. Do not stop to organize, edit, or judge any comments."

STEP 2: QUESTIONING PHASE

"Now, write down all of the questions you have. Try to keep up a constant stream of questioning for a full 5 minutes, and again, don't stop to edit or critique what you hear."

At this point, ask each of the groups to share one or two of their questions with the class. Usually, one of the first questions that comes up is, "What's under the question mark?"

STEP 3: HYPOTHESIS PHASE

"Let's narrow in on a specific question that many of you have probably wondered about. Given what you've just observed and shared, what do you as a group think *should* appear on the missing square? Back up your theory with evidence. How can you organize the pieces of information you gathered in Step 1 into a strong and logically consistent model?"

STEP 4: EXPERIMENTATION PHASE

"Scientific testing can be difficult and expensive to carry out, and it's limited by the types of technologies we have available. Pretend you have just enough funding and resources to carry out one simple experiment: You may reveal only *one* of the four corners of the unknown square. Choose carefully which corner you want to reveal, as some choices may be more informative than others, and you'll want to get the most bang for your buck. Once you have chosen, go ahead and lift up your corner." (For the lower elementary square, the only revelation option will be the color shade they see.)

STEP 5: HYPOTHESIS REVISION PHASE

"Is the result of your experiment consistent or inconsistent with your hypothesis? If it was consistent, did you gain any new information that can help you refine your existing model? If it was inconsistent, how would you revise your model to support this new information?"

STEP 6: PEER REVIEW PHASE

Ask each group to share one aspect of their model with the class, backing it up with their evidence. Then poll the class by asking: "Did any of you hear evidence for a model that was very different from your own, or that changed your way of thinking about the cube? Just as in the scientific community, we solve problems more effectively when we share openly and build on each other's ideas." Collect the squares at the end of the activity.

DO NOT REVEAL THE ANSWER.

Why not? Tell them this: "The world doesn't always cater to our desires, and it doesn't usually offer all the answers so easily. That restlessness and curiosity that you feel at the end of this activity is exactly what drives people to keep questioning, to keep experimenting, and to keep chipping away at understanding the universe a little bit better."

To extend the activity, ask students (or your colleagues) to design their own inquiry cubes.

FIGURE 8.2 ■ Kira's Cube for Middle and High School Students

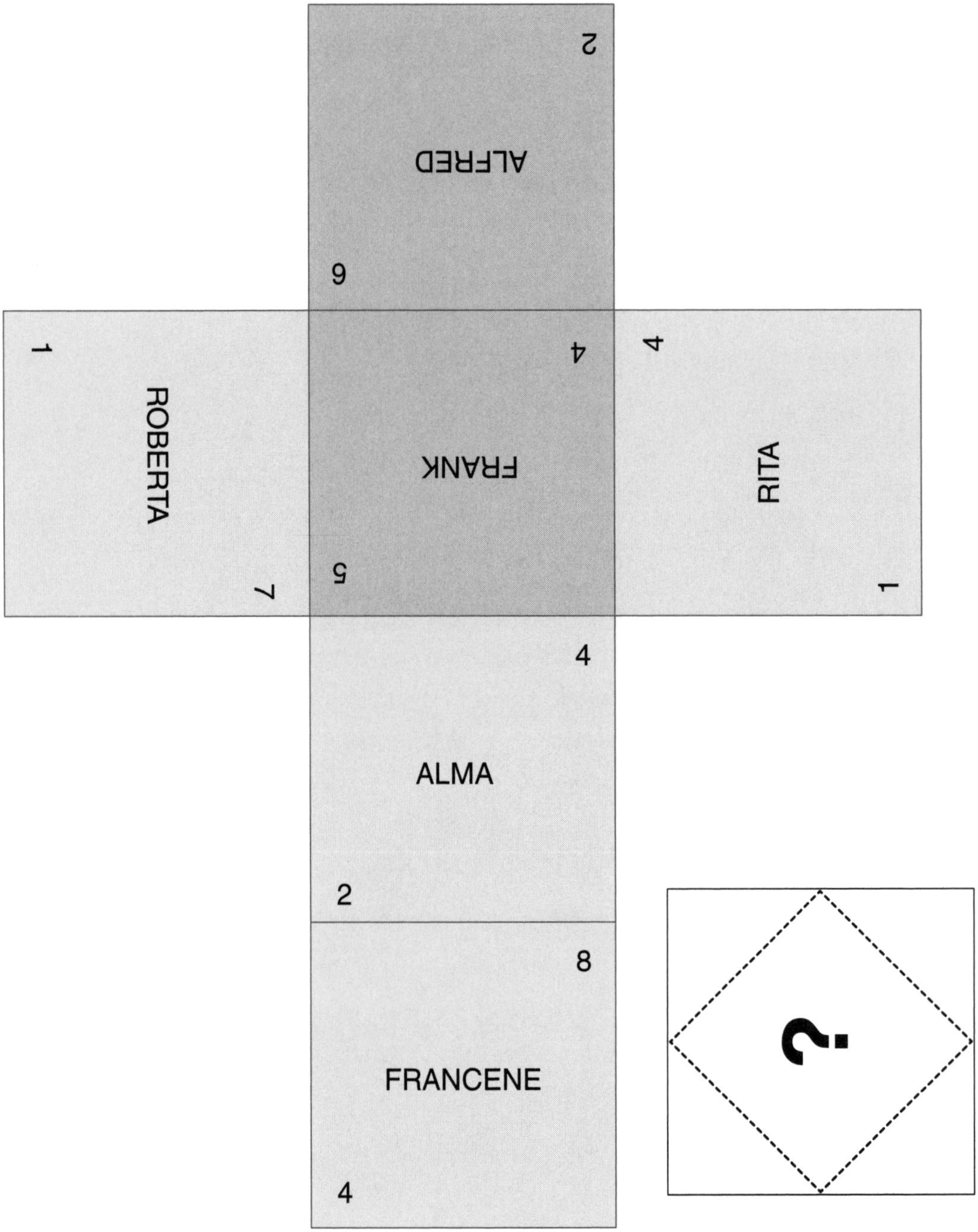

FIGURE 8.3 ■ Kira's Cube for Elementary Students

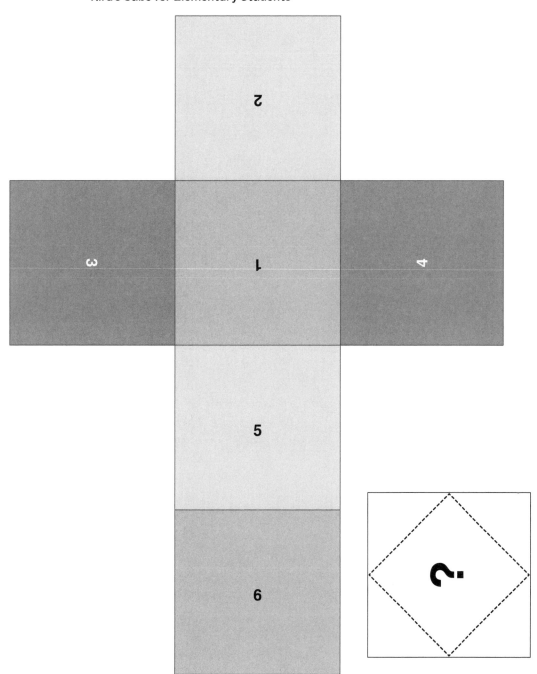

STRATEGY #5:
EXTEND THINKING TIME

"Thinking is a bit uncomfortable, but you'll get used to it. A matter of time and practice."

—Lloyd Alexander (1997)

Introduction to Extend Thinking Time

Teachers across the globe generally work within extreme time and space constraints. All too often this means we cram curricula, professional development, and stuff into schools. Have you ever watched teachers and students moving through schools: in the hallways, classroom, outside? It's as though there is an emergency happening. The energy of schools is one of intensity and business.

WE'VE BECOME SO CONCERNED
ABOUT THE TRAINS BEING ON TIME THAT
WE FORGET TO PICK UP THE PASSENGERS.

Not surprisingly, this often produces a suffocating and stressful environment, one in which it can be very hard to breathe, let alone learn. Kath Murdoch, in her moving TED Talk "The Power of Ummmm . . ." says:

> Classrooms are busy, often noisy, or strangely too quiet places. They can be very poor habitats for wonder.

These constraints can pose a challenge, yes. But they don't have to be a barrier to inquiry. We *can* turn "quick and decisive" classrooms into habitats of wonder and curiosity. There are small things (pausing, waiting, breathing, moving) and big things (offering choice, increasing student agency, utilizing technology) we can do to create the right environment for inquiry.

EXPERIENCE #40

How Do You Get Students to Think More?

Calling immediately on the first raised hand keeps the flow of a lesson moving, but can also shut down individual thinking. When we ask a question, and call on the first hand up, everyone else in the room is essentially "off the hook." Those students not called upon typically stop thinking because, well, somebody else has got it covered.

Wait time is an uncomfortable but necessary component of an inquiry classroom. Sometimes, just a few extra seconds can feel like an eternity. It takes time to think, articulate thoughts, and muster the courage to share. Education researcher Robert J. Stahl (1994) confirms that an optimal wait time is 3 to 5 seconds. Our average? Just 0.7 seconds!

HOW MANY SECONDS DO YOU THINK YOU WAIT ON AVERAGE BEFORE CALLING ON A STUDENT?

MY GUESS	THE REALITY

Now, let's find out how accurate your guess was. Film one of your lessons (or use the Earshot app). As you watch the video, look and listen for the first ten questions you ask and the time you wait before calling on a student. Calculate the number of seconds that go by. What's your actual average? Write it in the Reality Box and share with colleagues.

WAIT TIME TALLY

QUESTION	NUMBER OF SECONDS BETWEEN QUESTION AND ANSWER	STUDENT WHO ANSWERED
1.		
2.		
3.		
4.		
5.		
6.		
7.		
8.		
9.		
10.		

How accurate were you with your wait time guess?

What happened in those instances where you waited longer?

Who are your "eager speakers"? Did you call on them?

Which students, with a few more seconds, start to speak up?

 Available for download at **https://www.inquirypartners.com/**

EXPERIENCE #41

How Do You Get Students to Ask More Questions?

A Variation on The Question Formulation Technique[1]

Inquiry is all about asking questions and the exciting quest involved in answering them.

WHERE DOES THE WORD "QUESTION" COME FROM? A QUESTION IS A QUEST! CORNY, BUT TRUE.

For too long we've assumed that good questions will naturally spring from curious minds. Why take time to teach something that comes naturally? As natural as they may be, student-driven questions get squelched over time; they are driven underground by repressive environments or the fear of looking stupid. Teachers take over the question asking. Eventually, students forget that they even *have* questions of their own.

MAKE JUST ONE CHANGE: TEACH STUDENTS TO ASK THEIR OWN QUESTIONS

Inquiry classrooms require students to step back up to the plate, especially when it comes to asking questions. Questions unlock access to understanding and provide the impetus for working together in a democracy. Dan Rothstein and Luz Santana at The Right Question Institute spent over twenty years working alongside parents, students, and teachers to support question asking, eventually leading them to create the Question Formulation Technique (QFT) as outlined in their book, *Make Just One Change: Teach Students to Ask Their Own Questions* (2014).

Students *can* learn how to formulate great questions, and teachers can explicitly *teach* this skill. Like a muscle, question asking must be regularly exercised to grow stronger. The QFT is an evidence-based strategy for improving students' ability to formulate *their own* questions.

Yes, this exercise could easily go under the *Ask More; Talk Less* chapter. So why is it here? Asking questions *before rushing into answers* requires slowing down and extending thinking time. Allowing for more questions *before* jumping to answers can be extremely challenging. We've spent decades rewarding fast thinking. But fast isn't always best.

Can you hold back the questions you *wish* your students would ask? If you do, it will lead your students to more authentic student-driven inquiry and become a versatile strategy for building their research, critical thinking, and collaboration skills.

HERE'S HOW IT WORKS.

Start with a provocation, or what the QFT calls a Question Focus ("Q Focus"). For this first exercise, I will provide one for you and guide you through the process. As you go through, think about how you might adapt this for your classroom. What "Q Focus" might you use to introduce a new unit or get students to generate more questions on a topic? Is it an image, a sound, words, an experience?

> "WE NEED TO MAKE A STRONG, MORE DELIBERATE EFFORT TO BUILD THE CAPACITY OF ALL OUR CITIZENS TO THINK FOR THEMSELVES, WEIGH EVIDENCE, DISCERN BETWEEN FACT AND MYTH, DISCUSS, DEBATE, ANALYZE, AND PRIORITIZE."
>
> DAN ROTHSTEIN AND LUZ SANTANA

In a moment, you will look at an image on page 154. Your job is to write as many questions about that image as you can in 10 minutes.

RULES:

1. Number your questions (so you can refer to them quickly later on);

2. Don't stop to judge, edit, or comment on the questions;

3. Make sure everything written is phrased as a question, not a statement; and

4. Don't stop until the time is up.

Ready, Set, Questions!

FIGURE 9.1 ■ Try out the QFT using this Question Focus image.

$$25 - (3 + 1) \times 5$$

Source: A variation on the QFT. For more info about the full QFT go to www.rightquestion.org

You've got a list of questions, now it's time to sort and analyze them!

First, label each one of your questions as either "Closed" (a closed or convergent question has only one well-specified answer) or "Open" (an open or divergent question invites elaboration). This step is harder to do than it sounds. You will likely engage in some debates here. Decide on how you want to categorize each question (there is no "right" way). After labeling each question, look over your list as a whole. How many Closed and how many Open questions do you have? Where do they cluster? Is there a pattern?

Next, using the space below, choose one of your Closed questions and turn it into an Open question. Then, do the opposite.

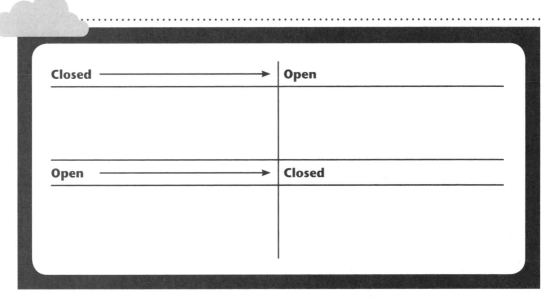

Closed ——————————▶ Open

Open ——————————▶ Closed

Read through your list one more time and choose *one* question that is most interesting to you (prioritization phase). If you are working as a team, try to get consensus on this one question.

MY/OUR FAVORITE QUESTION

Finally, exchange lists with someone else. After reading through their list, choose *your* favorite question from their list. Is it Open or Closed? What makes it your favorite?

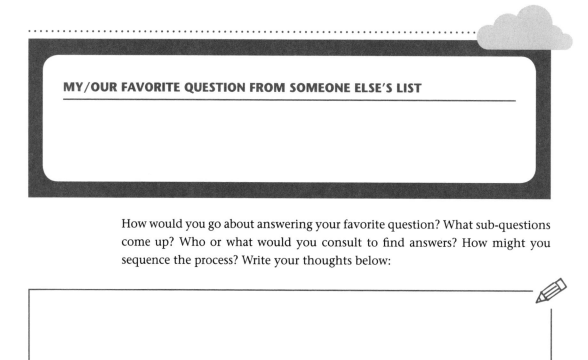

MY/OUR FAVORITE QUESTION FROM SOMEONE ELSE'S LIST

How would you go about answering your favorite question? What sub-questions come up? Who or what would you consult to find answers? How might you sequence the process? Write your thoughts below:

How might you use the QFT in your own classroom[3]?

Note

1   For more info about the full QFT, please read *Make Just One Change: Teach Students to Ask Their Own Questions* (2011) by Dan Rothstein and Luz Santana. I also encourage you to visit the resources listed on their website at www.rightquestion.org.

EXPERIENCE #42

How Do You Cede Control Without Losing It Completely?

Imagine flying a kite. The more string you give out, the higher the kite flies. Once up in the air, the kite requires little of you but a steady hand. You don't let go of the string. You wind it back in when necessary. It's the same with students and inquiry.

Authentic inquiry is fundamentally and necessarily learner driven. This doesn't mean, however, that it's a free-for-all. There must be conditions and structures in place in order for students to feel safe enough to explore and take risks.

Reflect on where and how you can "let out a little more string" in your classroom. Using the template on the next page, write down where you currently offer students choices in these areas. Share with a partner. Where could you open up even more opportunities for student choice? What needs to be in place to feel comfortable doing so?

The Control Kite Example

Spaces

When and how do your students choose who to work with or where to work?

How do students determine how they practice skills and gain information?

Topics

Do students have the opportunity to research problems and explore issues that interest them?

Tools and Products

How do you negotiate the use of tools, including technology?

Are students encouraged to locate their own sources of information?

Can students develop their own ways of demonstrating understanding?

Do students choose what to select for formative and summative assessment?

Time

How much time do you offer students to explore or create something on their own or in groups?

Can students start projects in nonlinear, creative ways?

The Control Kite Template

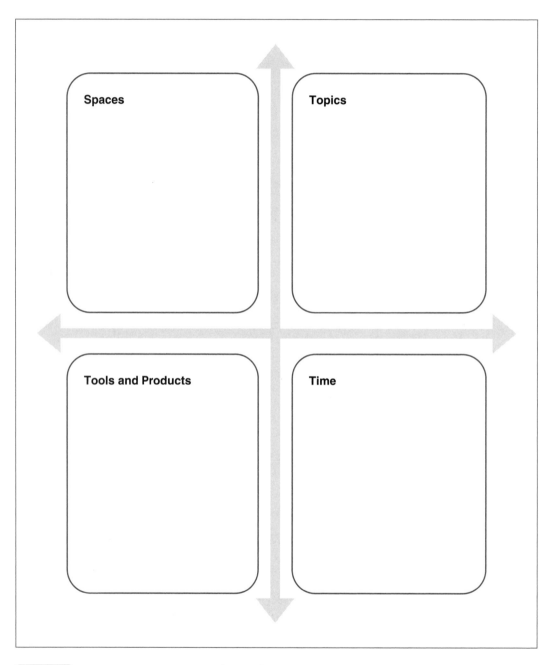

EXPERIENCE #43

How Do Inquiry and Mindfulness Connect?

Inquiry classrooms are balanced and harmonious. They build knowledge, skills, and dispositions in equal measure. Integrating mindfulness practices is incredibly helpful in rounding out dispositions of calm, community, and joy. Mindfulness practices offer great ways of extending thinking time and lowering stress levels (avoiding the "panic zone").

The positive benefits of meditation and mindfulness activities in the classroom are well-documented. Moments of silence, conscious breathing, and heightened awareness are all a part of the inquiry classroom. Inquiry and mindfulness? Hand in glove.

Eric Hoffman, a high school teacher, programmed a special bird call into his iPhone. He chose the loon, a bird that has at least four distinct sounds: the tremolo, wail, yodel, and hoot. Every 30 minutes, the loon's hoot calls out. It's one-note hoot is used to keep track of family, to make sure everyone's still doing OK. What a perfect choice for a classroom of students.

When Mr. Hoffman's loon calls, students pause their conversations and briefly stop whatever they are doing. They look up and around the room at one another. They take one deep breath in and one long exhale out. That's it. It takes no more than 10 seconds and makes a huge difference in their ability to relax and stay connected as a class.

What are the ways you reduce stress in your classroom?

EXPERIENCE #44

How Can You Support Innovative Student Thinking?

Inquiry demands creative, innovative thinking. It's not satisfying enough to unearth existing knowledge. Students need to be free to apply what they know to existing problems in new ways. How might we help build their capacity to innovate? Here are two of the most effective and simple ways I've found to support innovation with students (and colleagues).

WALKING BRAINSTORMS

The next time you introduce a problem or a question, get people out of their seats. Pair them up and invite them to walk around the perimeter of the school (or inside, if there is space), brainstorming possible approaches to answering the question or solving the problem. This should not take more than 10 minutes, but makes a huge difference in stimulating creativity. Why does this work so well? From a neurochemical perspective, our brains are more relaxed and open to new ideas when we physically move around. Plus, walking side-by-side breaks down barriers between people, strengthens emotional bonds, and loosens up hierarchical structures. Try this during a staff meeting or a PLC!

TWENTY PERCENT FREE TIME

Over the years, I've offered numerous inquiry workshops for teachers. The most powerful ones are only a couple of hours long. I simulate what it feels like to be a student in an inquiry classroom or demonstrate inquiry inside classrooms with teachers observing. There are times, however, when I've been asked to provide full-day or multi-day workshops. After a few hours, people are exhausted. Their eyes glaze over. They gravitate towards their smartphones. Done.

Oh, but I have so much more to tell them!

Moving forward with content and activities can often be like overwatering plants. At some point, people just need to soak it in. Rather than plugging ahead, I now offer at least one full hour during my 1-day workshops (approximately 20% of our time together, not including lunch) for teachers to use *however they wish*. Yes, I trust them to make good choices. They can meet in small grade-level or department teams, write in journals, call the plumber, answer email, take a long walk, start planning, respond to student writing. Workshop evaluations consistently rate the opportunity to use a chunk of time as they choose one of the most important parts of the day.

EXPERIENCE #45

How Do You Start Project-Based, Problem-Based, and Challenge-Based Learning?

The purpose of learning something should go well beyond passing a test or moving to the next grade level. We all know this, but this isn't the reality in most of our schools today. Without feeling like our work is significant in some way, we become compliant but not terribly curious. I was this way. I dutifully turned in my homework. I looked attentive in class as my mind wandered far, far away. I asked questions and made comments only to receive "participation points."

THIS MADE ME AN HONOR ROLL STUDENT BUT A TERRIBLE THINKER.

I remember those who didn't play the game of school as well. They wanted to solve real problems and engage in activities that held some purpose beyond getting a good grade. Ironically, these students are often seen, by themselves and others, as the underachievers. These purpose-focused students who are genuinely curious about solving big problems are in high demand today, however.

IN THE END, DON'T WE ALL WANT OUR EFFORTS TO MATTER?

Project-based learning (PBL) is rooted in the idea that knowledge, skills, and beliefs are best developed with authentic, contributive work that serves some purpose beyond school. Among other questions, PBL attempts to answer, "Why would I ever need to know this?" Like inquiry, PBL is often perceived as too challenging to implement in a traditional school setting. But just like inquiry, it's much easier than you think. Ready to demystify it?

Choose one of the ideas written in "The School Community" quadrant from Experience #17, "What is the Third Space?". Now, think of a genuine problem or project that needs to be solved or can be improved within your school context. How can your students be a part of examining and executing on a solution to this problem or project? Ask them to explore and share with you and one another. Write down your thoughts in the space provided.

Set up the expectations, carve out the time (20%), and let them go for it! That's it. You just got the PBL ball rolling. Want to keep it rolling, or roll it faster? Check out the Inquiry Resources for more ideas and great organizations focused on supporting PBL and experiential learning practices.

NOW WHAT?

Now that you've experienced inquiry yourself, it's time for some practical advice on how to implement it. Welcome to the "nuts-and-bolts" section!

This final chapter will help you plan for and assess inquiry. It will prepare you for the inevitable questions that come from parents and others unfamiliar with progressive teaching methods. Perhaps most importantly, it will help you mitigate issues arising from making time for inquiry.

EXPERIENCE #46

How Do You Plan for Inquiry?

Inquiry classrooms are magical places: creative, student driven, and dynamic. But when it's only the lesson you see unfolding, you're missing half the show. We cannot pretend that the magic of inquiry classrooms just happens, well, magically. Planning for inquiry reminds me of the following proverb:

A RIVER NEEDS BANKS TO FLOW.

Lesson plans are the proverbial banks. These banks provide the space and order necessary to encourage the freefall of ideas, divergent questions, and cognitive dissonance to take place. In fact, I've found that lesson planning is the most creative part of my job.

When I first started working with the International Baccalaureate program, writing detailed unit plans helped to make sure I was budgeting time for student questions. It also helped to remember that I needed to set aside time for students to choose which actions to take during a unit (realizing that sometimes *inaction* was the best option). When I design my lessons now, I go through each of these 5 steps, regardless of what or who I am teaching.

STEP 1: CONNECT WITH AND QUESTION THE CONTENT AS A PERSON, NOT AS A TEACHER.

Take off your teacher hat for a moment. How can you strengthen emotional bonds with and between your students within the context of this lesson? How can you share your own curiosity, doubts, and personality with students using the lesson as a vehicle? If the content isn't important, fascinating, and/or relevant to you, it's unlikely your students will find an emotional connection to it either.

- What questions still perplex and fascinate you?
- What relevant stories can you tell relating to the content?

- Are there metaphors that might be helpful to students?

- Do you remember the first time you learned this yourself?

- Are there websites that explore these questions and ideas in greater detail?

Here's how I might approach the first step for an upcoming lesson. Let's say I'm teaching Shakespeare's *Macbeth*, and we're on Act IV, Scene 1. You may remember this scene by its opening line: "Round about the cauldron go . . ." or it's repeated chorus: "Double, double, toil and trouble; Fire burn and cauldron bubble." It's an entire scene where witches create a complicated spell; full of challenging vocabulary and foreshadowing.

My emotional connection to the content:

This scene is bursting with strange and repulsive words—a recipe for disaster! It reminds me of potions class from the Harry Potter series. My husband is a former chef, and he always talks about the importance of getting the right ingredients. The process involved here reminds me of him in the kitchen; so incredibly detailed and painstakingly precise.

My lingering questions and wonders relating to the content:

- There are phrases in here that have been repeated for hundreds of years like "Double, double toil and trouble; Fire burn and cauldron bubble."

- Tons of rumors about the production issues haunted by prophesies. Why?

- How can a cauldron simultaneously boil and bake?

- How many times does the cat mew? Is the witch adding the number or repeating the previous witch? How do we know for sure?

- Why such a long scene describing this concoction?

- What's the difference between a spell and a charm?

Resources that will provide reliable and diverse perspectives on the content:

- Folger Shakespeare Library: https://www.folger.edu/macbeth

- Raphael Holinshed published his *Chronicles of England, Scotlande, and Irelande* in 1577. The second edition, published in 1587, was Shakespeare's primary reference work for most of his histories and many of his other plays, including *Macbeth*.

This "emotional brain dump" was fun and took me no more than 5 minutes to accomplish. In thinking through these things, I decided to share a personal anecdote about my husband in the kitchen (I think I even have an old photo of him in his chef outfit I can share). I will talk about how much he talks about the right ingredients being so important to the success of a dish. To get the students to connect with one another, I'll ask them to share their favorite dishes and analyze the ingredients that go into them (thinking about the role of ingredients in making a dish or a charm so special and memorable).

STEP 2: GET CLEAR ON THE GOALS AND ASSESSMENTS.

This is usually where we start when lesson planning: our objectives. Think about what you want students to get out of your lesson, and how you might measure these goals (even imperfectly). What mix of formative assessments will you use? Are there authentic assessments (products, performances, or presentations) that you can use to motivate them individually or in teams? What do you want the students know (content), be able to do (skills), and/or believe (dispositions) by the end of this lesson or unit?

Again, using the Shakespeare example, I might choose the following mix of content and skill-related objectives for my lesson. I try not to list more than five main objectives so that I can stay focused (less is more). I also really try to make sure I balance the knowledge, skills (especially communication, critical thinking, creativity, and collaboration), and dispositions (patience, empathy, growth mindset) when listing out my objectives.

WHAT WILL STUDENTS KNOW, DO, AND BELIEVE? (KNOWLEDGE, SKILLS, DISPOSITIONS)	HOW WILL WE KNOW WE'VE ACHIEVED THIS? (ASSESSMENTS)
Understand the scene's meaning (knowledge) CCSS.ELA-LITERACY.RL.11-12.4	Ingredient Analysis and Questions group presentation; listening in on conversations
Take risks with ideas; communicate clearly (skills)	Observations and student reflection survey

WHAT WILL STUDENTS KNOW, DO, AND BELIEVE? (KNOWLEDGE, SKILLS, DISPOSITIONS)	HOW WILL WE KNOW WE'VE ACHIEVED THIS? (ASSESSMENTS)
Back up conjectures with evidence (either from text, experience, or websites) CCSS.ELA-LITERACY.RL.11-12.1 (skills)	Ingredient Analysis (source citations)
Gain confidence and interest in tackling challenging texts like this one (dispositions)	Student reflection survey

STEP 3: DESIGN THE LESSON AND PLOT QUESTIONS.

Once I have a sense of the why and how, I am ready to create the flow. This is where traditional lesson planning comes in. What's your hook or anticipatory set? How much time do you think you'll need to provide instruction before releasing students? Will assignments be rigorous enough, but not completely out of reach? Will students be grouped together, when and how? How will students be held accountable for their work?

As you go through the lesson sequencing, you'll want to simultaneously think about the driving questions for this lesson (in the event that students don't raise these questions on their own during the lesson), as well as "pivot questions" that you can use to transition students to new activities or discussions. These questions are the ones you want students to really take time to think about. I often transfer these onto notecards and post them on the wall during a lesson and take them down as we address them. Students now alert me if there are questions still up on the wall.

STEP 4: CHECK FOR QUESTIONS, VOICE, AND CHOICE.

After mapping out the lesson flow and the driving questions, I go back through it to check for two important things: opportunities for student questions and student choice.

Now, look back through each of your activities to make sure that you've created time and opportunities for students to ask questions and make choices. Student voice (question asking) and student choice are the bedrock of inquiry classrooms, so make sure you're providing space and structure for these things. In my own lesson planning, I'd place an "X" next to activities that explicitly provide this. As mentioned before, there is no "rule" around how much or how many opportunities you provide, although I'd strive for a 50/50 balance between teacher-directed/teacher talk-time and student-directed/student talk-time.

Anybody who has spent any amount of time around a toddler knows that the easiest way to get buy-in and motivate forward motion is to offer choices, even limited ones. Choice is a key component of an inquiry classroom. Choice is about control, and in an inquiry classroom students are empowered to make choices that benefit their learning. As long as the choices are aligned with lesson objectives and classroom norms, they will add tremendous value to your classroom culture and student learning. Plus, the choices students make yield a lot of information for the teacher: information about how students see themselves, how well they can self-regulate, what and who they gravitate toward and away from.

As adults, we find all sorts of ways to wriggle out of uncomfortable situations. Most of us have choices; we can choose who we live with, where and whether we go to school or work, what we eat, when we sleep, whether we want to participate. Children aren't in this position. Having control over our own life is one of the many rewards of growing up. However, it makes it challenging to empathize with the experience of children.

Again, using the *Macbeth* example, here is what my lesson plan might look like at this point:

ACTIVITY/ TIMING	DRIVING QUESTION(S)	STUDENT QUESTIONS	STUDENT CHOICE
Personal Story (10 mins.)	What are the most important ingredients in your favorite dish? What do recipes have to do with this scene (connection)?		X
Reading and Review (5 mins.)	What does this scene leave you feeling? What questions does it raise for you?	X	

ACTIVITY/ TIMING	DRIVING QUESTION(S)	STUDENT QUESTIONS	STUDENT CHOICE
Group Task: Ingredient Analysis (15 mins.)	How easy, difficult, impossible, and/or immoral would it be to obtain each ingredient here today?		X
Small-Group Choice (10 mins.)	1) What's the most critical ingredient? Why? 2) How would you reverse the charm? 3) What ingredients may be missing?		X
Whole-Group Sharing (5 mins.)	Which words were confusing, and how did you find their definitions? Which choice question did you choose, and what did you come up with?		
Closing (5 mins.)	What kind of "prep work" for the charm needs to happen? What questions linger? (share my own)	X	

A NOTE ABOUT UNIT PLANNING

While this plan is designed for a lesson, you can easily adapt it for an entire unit. Rather than plotting out the activities in *minutes* during Step 3, simply extend them into the number of *days* allotted for your unit.

STEP 5: RAPIDLY REFLECT.

This step is often ignored, but it is a critical part of the inquiry cycle because it requires us as teachers to flex our reflective inquiry muscles! This step shouldn't require a lot of time, and it can always be completed with the students after a lesson or a unit—after all, they're some of your best evaluators, having engaged in the lesson from start to finish. Set a timer for 5 minutes and answer two simple questions:

- What went especially well?
- What would I change?

Here is what I wrote after trying out the *Macbeth* lesson:

What went well?

- Great engagement and discussions while sorting ingredients
- Twenty minutes was perfect amount of time for group projects

What would I change?

- Allow them to access websites to find definitions (reinforce source citing)
- Groups no larger than four people; otherwise students can disengage
- Shorten favorite recipe-sharing time

Going through this process helps me reflect on perennial questions like, Did students pursue the anticipated line of inquiry? Did they latch onto a misconception and refuse to let it go? Was everyone engaged; how do I know? Did students ask their own questions? Was there enough or too much student choice?

Successful inquiry classrooms may at times appear aimless and perhaps chaotic, but nothing could be further from the truth. Great inquiry lessons are actually some of the most carefully and thoughtfully planned learning events on the planet. Remember that a river needs banks to flow when thinking about guiding student inquiry. Be clear on why the river is flowing, where it's going, and how it will get there. The 5-Step Inquiry Lesson Plan will allow you to keep your knees bent and not fall over.

The 5-Step Inquiry Lesson Plan Template

STEP 1: GET PERSONAL.

My emotional connection(s) to the content:

My lingering questions and wonders relating to the content:

Resources that will provide reliable and diverse perspectives on the content:

STEP 2: GET CLEAR.

WHAT WILL STUDENTS KNOW, DO, AND BELIEVE? (KNOWLEDGE, SKILLS, DISPOSITIONS)	HOW WILL WE KNOW WE'VE ACHIEVED THIS? (ASSESSMENTS)

STEP 3: DESIGN THE PROCESS; PLOT THE QUESTIONS.

ACTIVITY/TIMING	DRIVING QUESTION(S)	STUDENT QUESTIONS	STUDENT CHOICE

STEP 4: DOUBLE-CHECK FOR STUDENT QUESTIONS AND CHOICE.

STEP 5: REFLECT.

What went well?	What would I change?

online resources Available for download at **https://www.inquirypartners.com/**

EXPERIENCE #47

How Do You Assess Inquiry?

Assessing student inquiry skills and dispositions can be accomplished in multiple ways. In the spirit of true inquiry, let me turn the question back to you: How can you assess each of these skills or dispositions in a formative way with your students? Extra rows at the end of the template are provided for additional skills and dispositions you feel are important to monitor and assess.

INQUIRY SKILL OR DISPOSITION	HOW MIGHT YOU ASSESS STUDENT PROGRESS IN THIS AREA?
Collaboration	
Question asking	
Critical analysis	
Problem solving	
Source citing	

INQUIRY SKILL OR DISPOSITION	HOW MIGHT YOU ASSESS STUDENT PROGRESS IN THIS AREA?
Self-reflection	
Offering feedback	

 Available for download at **https://www.inquirypartners.com/**

EXPERIENCE #48

How Do You Make Time for Inquiry?

This is a valid question. Inquiry requires more thinking, collaboration, and reflection time. What inquiry lacks in efficiency, it makes up for in effectiveness, assuming our goal is deep understanding, skills that endure, and dispositions that support a more peaceful world. Learning takes time.

Education author and international project-based learning (PBL) consultant Thom Markham (2016) writes, "[some] topics can't be taught, but must be learned through discovery, trial and error, or prototyping—all of which require more time." When Thom writes "taught," he's referring to direct instruction; the teacher-telling model.

While these activities are definitely a part of the inquiry classroom, we need to shift our thinking.

INQUIRY IS NOT AN EVENT TO BE SCHEDULED, BUT A WAY OF BEING IN THE CLASSROOM.

For me, inquiry is about how I view my role and the role of students. How I interact with my students doesn't require significantly more time, but a complete reorientation of how I *use* my time. We know the constraints and the standards up front. Sure, sometimes what is expected, and the time and support given to accomplish it, feels absurd.

This is where our creativity must come in. How do we take what we have, advocate for change, and create a learning experience worthy of our students' precious time?

Below is an example of how two teachers with the same objectives and time constraints might approach their lessons. What do you notice about their rhythm and structure? What is the role of the teacher and the students? How might you reorganize your time, so inquiry can happen without sacrificing your objectives?

TRADITIONAL CLASSROOM: 50 MINUTES	INQUIRY CLASSROOM: 50 MINUTES
5 minutes—teacher takes attendance; gets students to "settle in."	5 minutes—checking in with each other; attendance managed by students.
10 minutes—teacher goes over assigned homework with whole class.	10 minutes—teacher sets up small-group discussions and explains in-class project.
25 minutes—teacher explains a new concept to whole class, answering individual questions along the way.	10 minutes—small groups review assigned reading and discuss main ideas together.
5 minutes—students begin working in small groups; teacher consults with three groups during this time.	10 minutes—small groups transition to in-class project (student choice integrated); teacher consults with all six groups during this time.
5 minutes—group work is interrupted by teacher who needs to assign and explain new homework.	10 minutes—small groups present the in-class projects to whole class (includes 1-minute Q&A).
Teacher leads 45 minutes or 90% of the lesson.	5 minutes—students rapidly reflect using a tech polling platform.
	Teacher leads 15 minutes or 30% of the lesson.

Making time for inquiry is easier if students are well prepared to do the heavy lifting. Students at every age and stage need to be reminded and equipped to lead inside the classroom. After the first month of school, there should be an established rhythm to the class. You shouldn't need to stand in front of the class and be responsible for explaining everything. That is a time-waster; plus, it's boring and ineffective. Put your students in charge. *It's their pits, not yours, that should be sweaty at the end of the day!*

Take the first month together to establish routines and norms: how to establish groups, ask questions, join in discussions, and locate credible information. Practice and celebrate these skills and dispositions again and again throughout the year to reinforce student leadership. Try to make it so that management isn't your constant concern; deep thinking and cognitive challenge is.

One final note. You might see teachers lecturing in inquiry classrooms at times. Shocker! Again, it's that balance and harmony mantra. There is a time and a place for direct instruction and even (short) lectures. The point is that we need a better *balance*.

How do you make time for inquiry? Try it. Outline below the current rhythm of your day or a period, if you teach multiple classes. Where can you create more efficiencies? What routines will allow for more student talk, collaboration, and learner-driven work?

TIMING	TYPICAL ROUTINES

EXPERIENCE #49

How Do You Explain Inquiry to Skeptics?

There are valid concerns and real tensions with inquiry-based instruction in many schools. The often idealized and outdated vision of teaching and learning dies hard. If we let go of what we know, what might happen? The stakes of innovating feel too high.

How might you address these concerns with empathy and data? Respond to the following common concerns about inquiry. Share your responses with others and continue to refine them.

YOU'RE THE TEACHER. YOU SHOULD TEACH.

STUDENTS NEED TO GO THROUGH
THE CURRICULUM TO BE PREPARED FOR EXAMS.

INQUIRY WON'T PREPARE STUDENTS FOR THE REALITY
OF OUR CURRENT SCHOOL SYSTEM.

INQUIRY IS CHAOTIC.

INQUIRY DOESN'T TEACH THE BASICS.

INQUIRY TAKES TOO MUCH TIME.

online resources Available for download at **https://www.inquirypartners.com/**

EXPERIENCE #50

What Does Inquiry Look Like to You?

After going through the experiences in this book, how might you capture inquiry as an image? Pretend you are on assignment as a photojournalist. You've been asked to take the cover photo for this book. How might you capture and communicate "inquiry"?

Using your phone or a handful of colorful pens, take or make an image. Paste it below, then hang it up on a bulletin board with others, and/or share on social media using the hashtag *#ExperienceInquiry*.

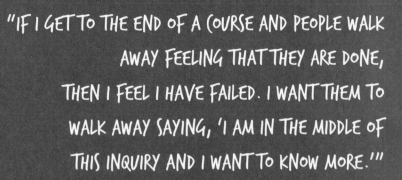

"IF I GET TO THE END OF A COURSE AND PEOPLE WALK AWAY FEELING THAT THEY ARE DONE, THEN I FEEL I HAVE FAILED. I WANT THEM TO WALK AWAY SAYING, 'I AM IN THE MIDDLE OF THIS INQUIRY AND I WANT TO KNOW MORE.'"

—KATHY SHORT, INQUIRY THOUGHT LEADER AND PROFESSOR, UNIVERSITY OF ARIZONA

What more do *you* want to know? List your questions in the space below. Sate your curiosity by consulting the resources provided in the next section.

11

INQUIRY RESOURCES

This book stands on the shoulders of inquiry practitioners I greatly admire and continue to learn from, many of whom have been mentioned throughout this book. Please supplement the experiences provided with some of my favorite thinkers, organizations, and resources for sparking interest, deepening understanding, and building the skills necessary to change classroom practice from traditional to inquiry based.

I challenged myself to pick no more than ten resources in each category, so what you see here is less of a "laundry list" and more of a "best in show." Please help update and curate this list by sharing your own inquiry resources. Be sure to periodically check back for updates, too, at

www.inquirypartners.com/ExperienceInquiry.

Kimberly's Top Ten Lists

INQUIRY BOOKS

1. ***Teaching as a Subversive Activity,*** **Neil Postman and Charles Weingartner**

The original inquiry manifesto written decades ago; also, the most dog-eared book in my education library. Still.

2. ***The Power of Inquiry,*** **Kath Murdoch**

Written by one of the most accessible writers and creative inquiry-based practitioners today.

3. ***Teaching with Your Mouth Shut,* Donald L. Finkel**

My favorite book on inquiry to recommend to college-level professors.

4. ***The Best Class You Never Taught,* Alexis Wiggins**

Written by the creator of Spider Web discussions (and daughter of beloved education thought leader, Grant Wiggins).

5. ***A More Beautiful Question,* Warren Berger**

A treatise on inquiry written by a gifted storyteller and compelling question asker.

6. ***Choice Words,* Peter H. Johnston**

A practical, inspiring book on why what we say matters.

7. ***Children's Inquiry,* Judith Wells Lindfors**

Dr. J. W. Lindfors' fascination of how students theorized about the world was ahead of its time.

8. ***Guided Inquiry,* Carol Kuhlthau, Leslie Maniotes, and Ann Caspari**

One of the best process and research-backed guides for implementing inquiry.

9. ***Make Just One Change: Teach Students to Ask Their Own Questions,* Daniel Rothstein and Luz Santana**

The importance of and the process for getting students to ask their own questions.

10. ***Redefining Smart,* Thom Markham**

A terrific treatise from an internationally focused, PBL pioneer.

INQUIRY VIDEOS AND PODCASTS

1. ***Teach Teachers to Create Magic,* Chris Emdin**

Professor Embdin from Columbia Teachers College urges educators to learn from the people who students learn the most from *outside of* formal education environments; pedagogical magic *can* be taught!

2. ***Five Principles of Extraordinary Math Teaching,* Dan Finkel**

This talk is nothing short of revolutionary. Each of the five principals are relevant to every inquiry classroom, regardless of subject or grade level. Dan's radio-style voice alone is worth a listen.

3. *The Power of Ummmm . . .*, **Kath Murdoch**

A compelling look at the environments that foster true curiosity ("wonder bubbles") and how to create them in the most unusual of places: the classroom. Part of this talk includes a short video of students' wonders; super cute!

4. *What's the Value of a Teacher*, **Alan November**

The rejoinder for this title should be ". . . in an age where information is plentiful, cheap and easy to come by?" Alan is a compelling and entertaining speaker on the importance of teaching media literacy skills.

5. *Who Owns the Learning?* **Most Likely to Succeed film**

Watch anxiously as a group of new ninth graders begin their first day in an inquiry-based setting. Observe how their teacher sets up a Socratic Seminar asking students to immediately take charge of their own learning.

6. *College Lectures Are about as Effective as Bloodletting*, **Carl Wieman**

Dr. Wieman is a Nobel Physicist from Stanford, and he doesn't mince words. Powerful evidence that active, student-led learning works.

7. *Three Rules to Spark Learning*, **Ramsey Musallem**

A chemistry teacher shares the life-threatening experience that saved him from "pseudo-teaching" for years.

8. *Oracy in the Classroom, School 21, London, England*

Watch as students learn to share ideas, back up their claims, and speak with purpose with sophistication rarely seen at such a young age.

9. *School in the Cloud*, **Sugata Mitra**

Innovator places a computer inside a wall in India. Magic unfolds as children in the village use nothing more than their own curiosity to make it function.

10. *Caine's Arcade*, **Caine Monroy**

Watch a 9-year-old create an elaborate arcade at his dad's auto parts store. Then cry with joy as the community comes to play!

INQUIRY ORGANIZATIONS

1. *Math for Love*

Math for Love teaches mathematics in its whole context. Mathematics begins by playing . . . with games, puzzles, patterns, shapes, numbers, structures, rules, and ideas. From there, you observe and ask questions. Owning your question leads to the rest: refinement, searching for solutions, discovering the connections that allow you to not just solve but understand your problem, and finally, rigorous writing and presentation of your solution.

2. *Galileo Educational Network*

The Galileo Educational Network creates, promotes, and disseminates innovative teaching and learning practices through research, professional learning, and fostering external collaborations.

3. *Liberating Structures*

Liberating Structures are easy-to-learn "microstructures" that enhance relational coordination and trust. They foster lively participating in groups of any size, making it possible to include and unleash everyone. Liberating Structures spark inventiveness by minimally structuring the way we interact while liberating content or subject matter.

4. *Youcubed*

Youcubed's goal is to inspire, educate, and empower teachers of mathematics, transforming the latest research on math into accessible and practical forms. Based on the latest research on how to teach math well and how to bring about high levels of student engagement and achievement.

5. *Visible Thinking*

Visible Thinking has a double goal: on the one hand, to cultivate students' thinking skills and dispositions, and, on the other, to deepen content learning. This means curiosity, concern for truth and understanding, a creative mindset, not just being skilled but also alert to thinking and learning opportunities and eager to take them.

6. *thinkLaw*

thinkLaw *helps educators* teach critical thinking to *all students* using real-life legal cases. They offer tools, guides, and coaching based on real-life cases. They find that the law's Socratic questions methods make it easy for teachers to ask questions that build student critical thinking skills. "Critical thinking should not be a luxury good."

7. *Edutopia*

Supported by Lucas Education Research, Edutopia is dedicated to transforming K–12 education so that all students can acquire and effectively apply the knowledge, attitudes, and skills necessary to thrive in their studies, careers, and adult lives. Founded by innovative and award-winning filmmaker George Lucas in 1991, they take a strategic approach to improving K–12 education.

8. *Critical Thinking Consortium*

The consortium's aim is to work in sound, sustained ways with educators and related organizations to inspire, support, and advocate for the infusion of critical, creative, and collaborative thinking as an educational goal and as a method of teaching and learning.

9. *Guided Inquiry Design (GID)*

GID helps students to think critically, make informed decisions, and know how to use the information available to learn new information and ideas, in order to create new knowledge. GID leverages the massive research from inquiry researcher and thought leader Dr. Carol Kuhlthau.

10. *Authentic Education*

The mission of Authentic Education, founded by the late, great Grant Wiggins, is to make schools better by providing clients with state-of-the-art educational thinking, tools, and training.

INQUIRY BLOGS

1. *What Ed Said*

whatedsaid.wordpress.com/

A prolific and concise blogger, Edna Sackson writes from the perspective of an International Baccalaureate (Primary Years) coach and elementary-level inquiry-focused practitioner. Founder of global community blog "Inquire Within" (inquiryblog.wordpress.com).

2. *Teach Thought*

teachthought.com

"It is our position that all learning should result in substantive personal and social change (as opposed to academic training)." Chock full of terrific podcasts from practitioners and thought leaders. Type "inquiry" in the search bar and have at it!

3. *Mind/Shift*

blogs.kqed.org/mindshift/

This San Francisco-based public news organization dedicates staff to smart journalism in education innovation. This is my "touchstone" site to find the best articles around inquiry and progressive education.

4. **Cult of Pedagogy**

   cultofpedagogy.com

Teacher nerds unite through this stylish blog and podcast created by Jennifer Gonzalez. You can learn how to pronounce the word *pedagogy* here!

5. **Atelierista**

   atelierista-anna.blogspot.com.au

Teacher Anna Golden documents her studio-style classroom with early learners, providing transcripts, photos, and easy-to-digest ideas. Poetic!

6. **Just Wondering**

   kathmurdoch.com.au

Kath's wonderings are provocative, honest, and refreshingly clear-eyed. She frequently shares her journeys to inquiry-based schools around the world, and actively solicits feedback from her community of readers.

7. **Time Space Education**

   timespaceeducation.wordpress.com

Thoughts on "Being purposeful, working from within, seeking simplicity, being timely, making friends with curriculum, understanding the power of mood, making space, and pursuing wisdom." Developed by and for classroom teachers.

8. **Innovative Inquirers**

   innovativeinquirers.weebly.com/blog

International inquiry teacher, Cindy Kaardal, does a terrific job of sharing how she manages time in an elementary classroom that favors student agency and integrates technology. Lots of fun photos to complement the text.

9. **A Teacher's Evolving Mind**

   http://www.natebowling.com

A brave and unabashedly honest look at teaching, policy, and politics written by an award-winning, equity-focused teacher.

10. **Chunk, Flip, Guide, Laugh**

   https://chunkflipguidelaugh.com

Nancy Bacon offers a structure for how people, especially adults, learn (andragogy)—and motivates us to take action.

APPENDICES

More Reasons to Fall in Love With Inquiry: the Inquiry Five (i5) and Alignment Documents

The i5 and Common Core State Standards

The i5 and Next Gen Science Standards

The i5 and Danielson Teaching Framework

The i5 and Marzano Framework

The i5 and Approaches to Teaching and Learning
(International Baccalaureate)

The i5 and High-Leverage Practices

Curriculum at-a-Glance Template (Southern Hemisphere)

THE I5 AND COMMON CORE STATE STANDARDS[1]

INQUIRY STRATEGY	APPLICABLE STANDARDS
Strategy #1: Get Personal	CCSS.ELA-LITERACY.CCRA.W.6 Use technology, including the Internet, to produce and publish writing and to interact and collaborate with others.
Strategy #2: Stay Curious	CCSS.ELA-LITERACY.CCRA.SL.1 Prepare for and participate effectively in a range of conversations and collaborations with diverse partners, building on others' ideas and expressing their own clearly and persuasively.
Strategy #3: Ask More, Talk Less	CCSS.ELA-LITERACY.CCRA.SL.6 Adapt speech to a variety of contexts and communicative tasks, demonstrating command of formal English when indicated or appropriate.
Strategy #4: Encourage Evidence	CCSS.ELA-LITERACY.CCRA.R.1 Read closely to determine what the text says explicitly and to make logical inferences from it; cite specific textual evidence when writing or speaking to support conclusions drawn from the text. CCSS.ELA-LITERACY.CCRA.R.8 Delineate and evaluate the argument and specific claims in a text, including the validity of the reasoning as well as the relevance and sufficiency of the evidence. CCSS.ELA-LITERACY.CCRA.W.1 Write arguments to support claims in an analysis of substantive topics or texts using valid reasoning and relevant and sufficient evidence. CCSS.ELA-LITERACY.CCRA.W.8 Gather relevant information from multiple print and digital sources, assess the credibility and accuracy of each source, and integrate the information while avoiding plagiarism.

INQUIRY STRATEGY	APPLICABLE STANDARDS
	CCSS.ELA-LITERACY.CCRA.W.9
	Draw evidence from literary or informational texts to support analysis, reflection, and research.
	CCSS.ELA-LITERACY.CCRA.SL.4
	Present information, findings, and supporting evidence such that listeners can follow the line of reasoning and the organization, development, and style are appropriate to task, purpose, and audience.
	CCSS.MATH.PRACTICE.MP3 Construct viable arguments and critique the reasoning of others.
Strategy #5: Extend Thinking Time	CCSS.ELA-LITERACY.CCRA.W.7
	Conduct short as well as more sustained research projects based on focused questions, demonstrating understanding of the subject under investigation.
	CCSS.ELA-LITERACY.CCRA.W.10
	Write routinely over extended time frames (time for research, reflection, and revision) and shorter time frames (a single sitting or a day or two) for a range of tasks, purposes, and audiences.
	CCSS.MATH.PRACTICE.MP1 Make sense of problems and persevere in solving them.

 Available for download at **https://www.inquirypartners.com/**

THE I5 AND NEXT GEN SCIENCE STANDARDS

INQUIRY STRATEGY	APPLICABLE STANDARD(S)
Strategy #1: Get Personal	Working as a team
Strategy #2: Stay Curious	Engaging in argument from evidence
Strategy #3: Ask More; Talk Less	Asking questions and defining problems
	Obtaining, evaluating, and communicating information
	Constructing explanations and designing solutions
Strategy #4: Encourage Evidence	Analyzing and interpreting data
Strategy #5: Extend Thinking Time	Planning and carrying out investigations
	Developing and using models

online resources ↘ Available for download at **https://www.inquirypartners.com/**

THE I5 AND DANIELSON TEACHING FRAMEWORK

INQUIRY STRATEGY	APPLICABLE DOMAIN(S)
Strategy #1: Get Personal	Domain 1.d: Demonstrating Knowledge of Resources
	Domain 3.a: Communicating With Students
	Domain 3.d: Demonstrating Flexibility and Responsiveness
Strategy #2: Stay Curious	Domain 2.a: Creating an Environment of Respect and Rapport
Strategy #3: Ask More, Talk Less	Domain 2.b: Establishing a Culture for Learning
	Domain 3.b: Using Questioning and Discussion Techniques

INQUIRY STRATEGY	APPLICABLE DOMAIN(S)
Strategy #4: Encourage Evidence	*This strategy is not explicitly addressed; however, the following Domain area is correlated as it asks students to self-assess and includes mention of addressing misunderstandings:* Domain 3.d: Using Assessment in Instruction
Strategy #5: Extend Thinking Time	Domain 1.e: Designing Coherent Instruction Domain 3.c: Engaging Students in Learning

 Available for download at **https://www.inquirypartners.com/**

THE I5 AND MARZANO FRAMEWORK

INQUIRY STRATEGY	OBSERVABLE CLASSROOM STRATEGIES AND BEHAVIORS
Strategy #1: Get Personal	1.3 Understanding students' interests and backgrounds (positive relationships) 2.1.3 Helps students to link prior knowledge to new content 2.6.1 Notices when students are not engaged 2.6.5 Maintains a lively pace 2.6.6 Demonstrates intensity and enthusiasm 2.6.8 Provides opportunities for students to talk about themselves
Strategy #2: Stay Curious	2.5 Probes typically underserved students' incorrect answers 5.6 Builds positive relationships with students by displaying objectivity and control

(Continued)

INQUIRY STRATEGY	OBSERVABLE CLASSROOM STRATEGIES AND BEHAVIORS
Strategy #3: Ask More, Talk Less	2.1.2 Organizes students in small groups to facilitate the processing of new knowledge
	2.4 Asks questions of typically underserved students with the same frequency and depth as other students
	2.6.3 Manages response rates
	2.6.7 Uses friendly controversy
	2.6.9 Presents unusual or intriguing information
Strategy #4: Encourage Evidence	2.2.5 Students examine errors in their own reasoning or the logic of information presented
	2.2.7 Students revise previous knowledge
Strategy #5: Extend Thinking Time	2.1.4 Breaks presentation of content and engages students in processing new information
	2.6.4 Uses physical movement
	5.1 Organizes a safe physical layout of the classroom to facilitate movement and focus on learning
	6.3 Provides students with the opportunity to self-reflect and track progress towards learning goal

 Available for download at **https://www.inquirypartners.com/**

THE I5 AND APPROACHES TO TEACHING AND LEARNING[2] (ATT/L)

INQUIRY STRATEGY	IB APPROACHES TO LEARNING SKILLS CATEGORIES
Strategy #1: Get Personal	Communication Skills: Exchanging thoughts, messages, and information effectively through interaction
	Social Skills and Collaboration Skills: Working effectively with others

INQUIRY STRATEGY	IB APPROACHES TO LEARNING SKILLS CATEGORIES
	Reading, writing, and using language to gather and communicate information
Strategy #2: Stay Curious	Affective and Reflection Skills: Managing state of mind; (re-)considering what has been learned; choosing and using ATL skills
Strategy #3: Ask More, Talk Less	Critical Thinking Skills: Analyzing and evaluating issues and ideas
	Creativity and Innovation Skills: Developing things and ideas that never existed before
	Transfer Skills: Utilizing skills and knowledge in multiple contexts
Strategy #4: Encourage Evidence	Research and Information Literacy Skills: Finding, interpreting, judging, and creating information
	Media Literacy Skills: Interacting with media to use and create ideas and information
Strategy #5: Extend Thinking Time	Self-Management and Organization Skills: Managing time and tasks effectively

 Available for download at **https://www.inquirypartners.com/**

THE I5 AND HIGH LEVERAGE PRACTICES[3]

INQUIRY STRATEGY	APPLICABLE PRACTICES
Strategy #1: Get Personal	Practice 10) Building respectful relationships with students
	Teachers increase the likelihood that students will engage and persist in school when they establish positive, individual relationships with them. Techniques for doing this include greeting students positively every day, having

(Continued)

INQUIRY STRATEGY	APPLICABLE PRACTICES
	frequent, brief, "check in" conversations with students to demonstrate care and interest, and following up with students who are experiencing difficult or special personal situations.
	Practice 7) Specifying and reinforcing productive student behavior
	Clear expectations for student behavior and careful work on the teacher's part to teach productive behavior to students, reward it, and strategically redirect off-task behavior help create classrooms that are productive learning environments for all. This practice includes not only skills for laying out classroom rules and managing truly disruptive behavior, but for recognizing the many ways that children might act when they actually are engaged and for teaching students how to interact with each other and the teacher while in class.
	Practice 11) Talking about a student with parents or other caregivers
	Regular communication between teachers and parents/guardians supports student learning. Teachers communicate with parents to provide information about students' academic progress, behavior, or development; to seek information and help; and to request parental involvement in school. These communications may take place in person, in writing, or over the phone. Productive communications are attentive to considerations of language and culture and designed to support parents and guardians in fostering their child's success in and out of school.
Strategy #2: Stay Curious	Practice 12) Learning about students' cultural, religious, family, intellectual, and personal experiences and resources for use in instruction
	Teachers must actively learn about their particular students in order to design instruction that will meet their needs. This includes being deliberate about trying to understand the cultural norms for communicating and collaborating that prevail in particular communities, how certain cultural and religious views affect what is considered appropriate in school, and the topics and issues that interest individual students and groups of students. It also means keeping

INQUIRY STRATEGY	APPLICABLE PRACTICES
	track of what is happening in students' personal lives so as to be able to respond appropriately when an out-of-school experience affects what is happening in school.

Practice 19) Analyzing instruction for the purpose of improving it

Learning to teach is an ongoing process that requires regular analysis of instruction and its effectiveness. Teachers study their own teaching and that of their colleagues in order to improve their understanding of the complex interactions between teachers, students, and content and of the impact of particular instructional approaches. Analyzing instruction may take place individually or collectively and involves identifying salient features of the instruction and making reasoned hypotheses for how to improve. |
| Strategy #3: Ask More, Talk Less | **Practice 1) Leading a group discussion**

In a group discussion, the teacher and all of the students work on specific content together, using one another's ideas as resources. The purposes of a discussion are to build collective knowledge and capability in relation to specific instructional goals and to allow students to practice listening, speaking, and interpreting. The teacher and a wide range of students contribute orally, listen actively, and respond to and learn from others' contributions.

Practice 3) Eliciting and interpreting individual students' thinking

Teachers pose questions or tasks that provoke or allow students to share their thinking about specific academic content in order to evaluate student understanding, guide instructional decisions, and surface ideas that will benefit other students. To do this effectively, a teacher draws out a student's thinking through carefully chosen questions and tasks and considers and checks alternative interpretations of the student's ideas and methods. |

(Continued)

INQUIRY STRATEGY	APPLICABLE PRACTICES
	Practice 9) Setting up and managing small group work
	Teachers use small group work when instructional goals call for in-depth interaction among students and in order to teach students to work collaboratively. To use groups effectively, teachers choose tasks that require and foster collaborative work, issue clear directions that permit groups to work semi-independently, and implement mechanisms for holding students accountable for both collective and individual learning. They use their own time strategically, deliberately choosing which groups to work with, when, and on what.
Strategy #4: Encourage Evidence	Practice 5) Implementing norms and routines for classroom discourse and work
	Each discipline has norms and routines that reflect the ways in which people in the field construct and share knowledge. These norms and routines vary across subjects but often include establishing hypotheses, providing evidence for claims, and showing one's thinking in detail. Teaching students what they are, why they are important, and how to use them is crucial to building understanding and capability in a given subject. Teachers may use explicit explanation, modeling, and repeated practice to do this.
Strategy #5: Extend Thinking Time	Practice 14) Designing single lessons and sequences of lessons
	Carefully sequenced lessons help students develop deep understanding of content and sophisticated skills and practices. Teachers design and sequence lessons with an eye toward providing opportunities for student inquiry and discovery and include opportunities for students to practice and master foundational concepts and skills before moving on to more advanced ones. Effectively sequenced lessons maintain a coherent focus while keeping students engaged; they also help students achieve appreciation of what they have learned.

 Available for download at **https://www.inquirypartners.com/**

Notes

1   Anchor Standards for Reading, Speaking, Listening, and Language; Standards for Mathematical Teaching

2   The International Baccalaureate Organization

3   TeachingWorks, University of Michigan

CURRICULUM AT-A-GLANCE (SOUTHERN HEMISPHERE)

FEBRUARY	MARCH
APRIL	**MAY**
JUNE	**JULY**
AUGUST	**SEPTEMBER**
OCTOBER	**NOVEMBER**

 Available for download at **https://www.inquirypartners.com/**

REFERENCES

Alexander, L. (1997). *The iron ring*. London, UK: Puffin Books

Alrø, H., & Johnsen-Høines, M. (2012). Trenger en å spørre for å være spørrende? (Inquiry without posing questions?). *The Mathematics Enthusiast*, 9(3), 255. The University of Montana.

Bruner, J. (1986). *Actual minds, possible worlds*. Cambridge, MA: Harvard University Press.

Dewey, J. (1938). *Experience & education*. New York, NY: Macmillan.

Finkel, D. L. (2000). *Teaching with your mouth shut*. Portsmouth, NH: Boynton-Cook Publishers.

Francis, E. M. (2016). *Now that's a good question!* Alexandria, VA: ASCD.

Kuhlthau C., Maniotes L., & Caspari A. (2012). *Guided inquiry design*. Santa Barbara, CA: ABC-CLIO Publishers.

Lindfors, J. W. (1999). *Children's inquiry: Using language to make sense of the world*. New York, NY: Teachers College Press.

Markham, T. (2016). *Redefining smart*. Thousand Oaks, CA: Corwin Press.

Marzano, R. J. and Simms, J. A. (2014). *Questioning sequences in the classroom*. Bloomington, IN: Marzano Research.

Postman, N., & Weingartner, C. (1969). *Teaching as a subversive activity*. New York, NY: Dell Publishing.

Rothstein, D., & Santana, L. (2014). *Make just one change: Teach students to ask their own questions*. Cambridge, MA: Harvard Education Press.

Short, K. G. (1997, May/June). Inquiring into inquiry. *Learning Magazine*.

Stahl, R. J. (1994). Using "think-time" and "wait-time" skillfully in the classroom. *ERIC Digest*.

Wiggins, G. (1998). *Educative assessment*. San Francisco, CA: Jossey-Bass.

Zenger, J., & Folkman, J. (2016, July 14). What great listeners actually do. *Harvard Business Review*.

INDEX

A SAGE Publishing Company

Helping educators make the greatest impact

CORWIN HAS ONE MISSION: to enhance education through intentional professional learning.

We build long-term relationships with our authors, educators, clients, and associations who partner with us to develop and continuously improve the best evidence-based practices that establish and support lifelong learning.

Confident Teachers, Inspired Learners

No matter where you are in your professional journey, Corwin aims to ease the many demands teachers face on a daily basis with accessible strategies that benefit ALL learners. Through research-based, high-quality content, we offer practical guidance on a wide range of topics, including curriculum planning, learning frameworks, classroom design and management, and much more. Our suite of books, videos, consulting services, and online resources, developed by renowned educators, are designed for easy implementation and to provide you AND your students with tangible results.

James Nottingham and Bosse Larsson

Create the right conditions for a growth mindset to flourish in your school and your students.

James Nottingham

Embrace challenge and celebrate eureka!

Carla Marschall and Rachel French

Develop a thinking classroom that helps students move from the factual to the conceptual.

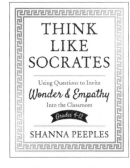

Shanna Peeples

The key to creating wonder and empathy in class? Questions!

Lisa Westman

Build collaborative student–teacher relationships as a precursor to student growth.

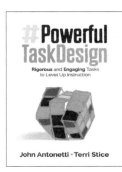

John Antonetti and Terri Stice

Analyze, design, and refine engaging tasks of learning.

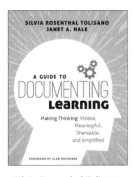

Silvia Rosenthal Tolisano and Janet A. Hale

Discover a new approach to contemporary documentation and learning.

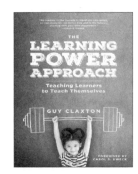

Guy Claxton

Become mind-fit for life!

CORWIN